TAX POLICY
AND THE ECONOMY   6

edited by ***James M. Poterba***

National Bureau of Economic Research
The MIT Press, Cambridge, Massachusetts

Send orders and business correspondence to:
The MIT Press
55 Hayward Street
Cambridge, MA 02142

In the United Kingdom, continental Europe, and the Middle East and Africa, send orders and business correspondence to:
The MIT Press Ltd.
14 Bloomsbury Square
London, WC1A 2LP
ENGLAND

ISSN: 0892-8649
ISBN: hardcover 0-262-16130-3
       paperback 0-262-66077-6

Library of Congress number 87-644377

Since this volume is a record of conference proceedings, it has been exempted from the rules governing critical review of manuscripts by the Board of Directors of the National Bureau (resolution adopted 8 June 1948, as revised 21 November 1949 and 20 April 1968).

CONTENTS

INTRODUCTION

James M. Poterba
MIT and NBER

The specter of an election-year recession has brought tax reform, or more accurately tax reduction, to the center stage of policy debate. Only five years after thinking that the Tax Reform Act of 1986 would end discussions of tax reform for at least a decade, virtually all of the issues from 1986—tax incentives for saving, the structure of marginal tax rates, capital gains relief, and the investment tax credit—are being reconsidered. The debates turn critically on economic analyses of the incentive, distributional, and efficiency effects of potential reforms. These are precisely the issues that are considered in the papers in this volume.

In November 1991, NBER researchers met in Washington, D.C., for the sixth annual Tax Policy and the Economy conference. This conference is designed to facilitate interaction between academic researchers and the tax policy community, and to present research findings that are relevant to current policy discussions. The five papers in this volume present new research results that have an important bearing on personal and corporate tax policy.

The first paper, "Government Policy and Retirement Saving" by Steven Venti and David Wise, considers the hotly debated question of whether universal IRAs in the early 1980s encouraged personal saving. Venti and Wise present new data from household surveys to show that most of the households who contributed to IRAs had limited non-IRA assets. This argues against the view that IRA contributions were simply transfers from other tax-disfavored saving vehicles. They also show that the financial holdings of IRA contributors grew much faster than those of noncontributors, again suggesting that IRAs were successful in encouraging personal saving.

My paper, "Why Didn't the Tax Reform Act of 1986 Raise Corporate Taxes?," studies the behavior of corporate tax receipts since 1986. The Tax Reform Act of 1986 was projected to raise corporate taxes by more than $120 billion over the 1986 to 1991 period. Actual federal corporate tax receipts in the last five years have fallen far short of these projections. The paper explores the factors that contributed to this shortfall. The most important is lower-than-expected corporate profits. The predicted rates of corporate profits when the 1986 Tax Reform Act was enacted were high by historical standards, and the U.S. economy in the late 1980s did not experience total returns on corporate capital as high as the forecasts would have suggested. This reduction in pretax returns has been compounded by an increase in corporate interest payments as a share of corporate operating income, and a rise in the income reported through S rather than C corporations, in the years since 1986. Both of these changes are likely to be due in part to the changes in tax incentives in the 1986 Tax Reform Act.

Lawrence Goulder's paper considers "Carbon Tax Design and U.S. Industry Performance." The carbon tax is the policy instrument most frequently suggested as a means to reduce U.S. emissions of carbon dioxide as part of a global campaign to reduce the potential problem of global warming. Goulder's paper uses a sophisticated general-equilibrium model of the U.S. economy to study how different ways of implementing a carbon tax would affect different industries. The results suggest that the burden of a carbon tax will be highly concentrated on a few industries involved in production or heavy utilization of carbon fuels. The precise cost of the carbon tax for a given industry, however, is quite sensitive to whether the tax is imposed on production of carbon fuels or on the consumption of these fuels. Goulder also demonstrates that many of the distortionary effects of the carbon tax could be offset by using the revenues from the tax to reduce the rates of existing distortionary taxes.

The fourth paper, by Joel Slemrod, presents important information on income inequality, an increasingly focal issue in tax policy debate. In "Taxation and Inequality: A Time Exposure Perspective," Slemrod uses data from a data set that follows the same taxpayers in several successive years. He finds that the federal income tax slightly reduces inequality. The equalizing effect of the tax system has not changed significantly over time, according to Slemrod's results. The inequality of pre-tax and post-tax incomes has, nevertheless, risen sharply during the last two decades, largely as a result of increasingly unequal distribution of wage and salary income. In contrast to previous studies, which argue that annual income varies for a variety of transitory reasons, Slemrod finds that conclusions about inequality are not significantly affected by focusing on a household's average income over a period of several years.

The final paper, by Alan Auerbach, Jagadeesh Gokhale, and Laurence Kotlikoff, examines "Social Security and Medicare Policy from the Perspective of Generational Accounting." These authors have developed a powerful analytical tool, generational accounting, for synthesizing the effects of complex tax and expenditure policies on individuals of different ages. They apply their framework to study how current proposals for changing the benefits and financing of transfer programs to the elderly, Medicare and Social Security, would affect the welfare of current and future generations. They find that continuation of current trends in Medicare spending, or the failure to accumulate a substantial Social Security trust fund, can substantially alter the intergenerational distribution of the burdens implied by current transfer programs. Either of these scenarios would shift much larger tax burdens to future generations than current policy, or more optimistic assumptions about health care costs, suggest.

The research presented in this volume exemplifies the important interaction between policy-making and academic research. NBER researchers take many of their cues for topics to study from the ongoing tax policy debates in Washington and state capitals. In return, much of the statistical and analytical work that provides the basis for tax policy debates is the result of academic research. The quality of the research presented at this year's Tax Policy and the Economy meeting suggests that this symbiotic tradition is alive and well.

ACKNOWLEDGMENTS

The authors and I are indebted to those who made this volume, and the conference that preceded it, a reality. NBER President Martin Feldstein, and Executive Director Geoffrey Carliner, have been enthusiastic supporters of the Tax Policy and the Economy conference since it began six years ago. Candace Morrissey assisted throughout the preparation of this volume. Kirsten Foss Davis, the NBER's Conference Director, Ilana Hardesty, and Lauren Lariviere organized the conference logistics with their almost-legendary efficiency and good cheer. I am personally grateful to the authors for agreeing to write papers that are explicitly geared to the wide dissemination of research findings, rather than to presentation of detailed findings to a narrow technical audience, and for their prompt attention to my editorial requests.

GOVERNMENT POLICY AND PERSONAL RETIREMENT SAVING

Steven F. Venti
Dartmouth College and NBER

David A. Wise
J.F. Kennedy School of Government, Harvard University and NBER

Incentives to save for retirement have been an important component of government tax policy since the Revenue Act of 1942 made employer pension contributions tax-deductible. Since that time, pension funds have grown enormously. Private firm pension assets increased from $13 billion in 1950 to $1,836 billion in 1989.[1] But only about half of the work force is covered by a pension plan and thus benefit from this inducement to employers to save for their employees' retirement. To address this inequity and to provide a retirement saving incentive for employees not covered by pension plans, the Individual Retirement Account (IRA) was introduced in 1974. Under this plan, employees without an employer-provided pension plan could put up to $1,500 each year in an IRA account. The contribution was tax-deductible and the return on the balance accumulated tax free. Taxes were paid on withdrawal. The non-

We are grateful to Art Kennickell for providing a cleaned version of the SCF data set (Avery and Kennickell, 1988). Some of the CES and SIPP data were made available by the Inter-University Consortium for Political and Social Research. We are grateful to Angus Deaton, Alan Gustman, James Poterba, Jonathan Skinner, and Richard Thaler for their comments on earlier drafts of the paper. Financial support was provided by the National Institute of Aging, grant number PO1 AG05842-06

[1] Including government pension funds the total was $2,786 billion in 1989.

employed spouse of an employee could contribute up to $250 per year. The self-employed were covered by Keogh plans introduced in 1962. The Economic Recovery Tax Act of 1981 extended the IRA to all employees beginning in 1982. In addition, the contribution limit, which was increased to $1,750 in 1977, was raised to $2,000.

The 1981 legislation sparked a wave of promotion by IRAs by banks and other financial institutions. IRA (and Keogh) assets grew from $39 billion in 1981 to almost one-half trillion by 1989 (see Piacentini and Cerino, 1990). By 1989, IRA assets were equal to 27 percent of firm pension plan assets, an increase from only 4 percent in 1981. About 30 percent of households had IRA accounts by 1986. After firm pension plans, IRAs seemed destined to become the principal form of saving for retirement. IRAs are the focus of this paper. More recently there has been an explosion in 401(k) plans that do not have income restrictions and have higher contribution limits.

Largely because of their tax cost, IRAs were a major topic of discussion prior to passage of the Tax Reform Act of 1986. The original "Treasury I" plan proposed that the annual contribution limit be raised to $2,500 and that the spousal contribution be raised from the $250 to $2,500. The Senate Finance Committee proposed that the existing plan be eliminated. The compromise solution left the existing plan intact for families with incomes less than $40,000, for single persons with incomes less than $25,000, and for all persons not covered by a firm pension plan. For those with a pension plan, the tax deduction of the contribution was phased out between $40,000 and $50,000 for families and between $25,000 and $35,000 for single persons. Even persons with incomes above these limits could contribute to an IRA without the tax deduction and the returns accumulated tax free, with the tax to be paid on withdrawal.

The Tax Reform Act of 1986 eliminated the tax deduction for about 15 percent of the 1985 contributors and partially restricted the deduction for another 12 percent (see Employee Benefit Research Institute, 1986). But the number of contributors and the amount contributed fell much more than these figures would suggest. The total amount deducted dropped from $37.8 billion to $14.1 billion, a 62.8 percent decline.[2] This "overreaction" is at least in part attributable to widespread misunderstanding of the legislation (often reported at the time to have eliminated IRAs) and to the marked decline in the promotion of IRAs. Indeed, a recent survey revealed that about half of all persons eligible for an IRA deduction

[2] The percent of tax returns showing an IRA deduction fell from 15.1 percent in 1986 to 6.8 percent in 1987, a 55.0 percent decline.

following the 1986 legislation mistakenly believed they were no longer eligible. (*IRA Reporter*, 1988).

The debate surrounding the 1986 legislation raised questions about the distribution of accounts by income and about the net saving effect of the accounts.[3] The latter question has led to the most extensive empirical research. An early paper by Hubbard (1984) using a 1979 survey conducted for the President's Commission on Pension Policy suggested that IRAs stimulated new saving prior to 1982. He found that contributions to IRAs and Keoghs, unlike "saving" through private pensions or Social Security, increase household net worth, given permanent income and other household characteristics. In a series of papers based on the 1983 Survey of Consumer Finances, the Survey of Income and Participation, and the Consumer Expenditure Surveys, Venti and Wise (1986, 1987, 1990a, 1991a) concluded that additional IRA contributions represented "new" saving for the most part. Feenberg and Skinner (1989), using a 1980 to 1984 panel of taxpayers, found that IRA contributors increased their saving over time by more than noncontributors even after controlling for initial wealth. They were unable to find substitution of IRA for non-IRA saving. Gale and Scholz (1990), based on the 1986 Survey of Consumer Finances, concludes that most IRA saving is not new saving, but rather represents saving that otherwise would have occurred in other forms. Joines and Manegold (1991), using a taxpayer panel, offer a middle-ground estimate. All of the studies agree that about $0.30 to $0.35 of each dollar put in an IRA account is funded by reducing taxes. The various Venti and Wise estimates suggest that $0.45 to $0.66 of each dollar comes from reducing consumption expenditure, the Feenberg and Skinner estimates imply that about two-thirds of each dollar comes from reduced consumption, the Gale and Scholz estimates are from −$.02 to $0.25, and the Joines and Manegold "best guess" is $0.305.

The goal of this paper is not to review these studies, although such an endeavor would certainly be worthwhile. Instead, we present in a simple format the basic patterns of IRA and non-IRA saving behavior, without the constraints imposed by the more formal models, some of which are rather complex.

The paper begins with a review of the level of personal saving in the United States and a discussion of the distribution of IRA accounts by age

---

[3] The proponents of the original 1974 IRA legislation emphasized the savings inducement for persons not covered by private pension plans. But whether this goal has been met has received little recent attention. We found in earlier work (Venti and Wise, 1988) that it was not. After controlling for individual attributes such as age and income, we found that persons without pension plans are no more likely than persons with pensions to contribute to an IRA account.

and income. The data suggest that at least 40 percent of households would have opened an IRA account over the course of their lives under the pre-1986 legislation. At least 60 percent of households with incomes above $30,000 would have opened accounts. Evidence on the saving effects of IRAs is presented in sections II through IV. The exposition is primarily graphical. Although the analysis is nontechnical, by considering several types of data we attempt to account for factors, such as individual propensity to save, that may confound the interpretation of the data. We find that the data provide little support for the possibility that IRAs had no net saving effect. Finally, we comment on the simple theoretical model that has led some observers to conclude that IRAs had no saving effect. We conclude that this simple model does not capture the prominent features of IRA saving and thus that its implications are unlikely to be valid. In particular, the assumption that IRA saving and other saving are treated by actual decision makers as perfect substitutes is inconsistent with the empirical evidence.

I. BACKGROUND

Most of the data discussed here pertain to IRA contributions, IRA asset balances, and non-IRA asset balances. The data are from three sources: the Consumer Expenditure Surveys (CESs) for 1980 through 1989, the Survey of Income and Program Participation (SIPP) for 1985 through 1987, and the Survey of Consumer Finance (SCF) for 1983 and 1986. Although much of the data in the three surveys is overlapping, the exact coverage and definitions differ among the surveys. The CES data span the period before and after the IRA program. They provide data on non-IRA asset balances and on IRA contributions in each year, but not on IRA balances. Both the SIPP and the SCF provide detailed information on non-IRA asset balances and IRA balances, but not on IRA contributions. The household is the unit of analysis for the CES and the SCF data; the SIPP data allow analysis based on household and family units. The family is the more appropriate unit because it corresponds to the typical IRS tax filing unit. For comparability, however, we present household data in most instances. For all the analyses in this paper a household or family is excluded if either the respondent or the spouse of the respondent is self-employed. The self-employed had access to Keogh plans with very different contribution limits than IRAs. In most cases IRAs were not a feasible option for the self-employed. Elimination of the self-employed also minimizes a potential complication that arises because two of the surveys (the CESs and the 1986 SCF) ask respondents for combined IRA and Keogh balances. Some details of each of the data sets are presented in the Appendix.

A. *Low Personal Saving in the United States*

On the eve of retirement the typical American family has only about $6,600 in financial assets. Personal saving in the United States has declined substantially as a fraction of personal income since the early 1950s and a large proportion of families reach retirement age with little or no personal saving. Personal saving declined from between 3% and 6% of disposable private income in the 1950s to around 1 percent in the early 1980s, based on computations made by Summers and Carroll (1987).[4] These numbers are adjusted for inflation and exclude saving by employers through defined-benefit pension plans.[5] Without the inflation adjustment, the downward trend begins only after 1973.

Aggregate saving rates, of course, reflect the wealth accumulation of all households, some of whom save very large amounts. Micro data show that a large fraction of families have almost no personal saving. Based on the recent Survey of Income and Program Participation (SIPP), we (Venti and Wise 1991a) computed the composition of total wealth for all households in 1984. The results are summarized in Figure 1. The amounts reflect median wealth by asset category.[6] It is clear that most families approach retirement age with very little personal saving other than housing equity. Among households with heads aged 60 to 65, median liquid wealth is only $6,600; the median value of housing equity is $43,000.[7] The majority of families rely heavily on Social Security benefits for support after retirement, and to a much more limited extent on the saving that is done for them by employers through defined-benefit pension plans.[8]

---

[4] Many other studies using different definitions of saving have reported a similar downward trend. See for example, Bosworth, Burtless, and Sabelhaus (1991).

[5] The National Income Accounts include firm contributions to defined-benefit pension plans under "personal saving." Inflation-adjusted saving is measured saving, minus the inflation rate (the GNP deflator), times net interest-bearing assets.

[6] Thus the component medians do not sum to the median of total wealth.

[7] Liquid wealth is broadly defined to include interest earning assets held in banks and other institutions, mortgages held, money owed from sale of businesses, U.S. Savings Bonds, and checking accounts, equity in stocks and mutual fund shares, less unsecured debt. Other wealth includes net equity in vehicles, business equity, and real estate equity (other than owned home).

[8] The SIPP data allow estimation of the value of Social Security and pension plan benefits only after the payments are received. Thus wealth in the form of Social Security and pensions is only recorded for persons who have begun to receive the payments. The median of Social Security and pension wealth combined is $113,400 (the median of Social

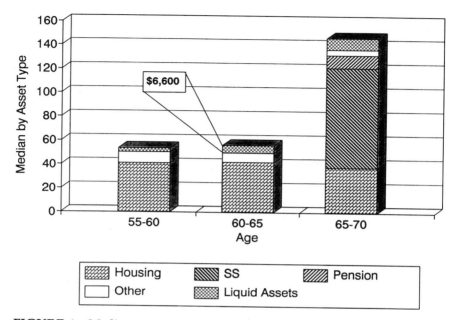

FIGURE 1. *Median asset balance by age and type of asset.*

B. IRA Assets and The Distribution of Accounts by Age and Income

The explosion of IRA saving after the 1981 legislation can be judged by comparing assets in IRA accounts to firm pension fund assets, reflecting the retirement saving by firms for their employees. The aggregate data are graphed in Figure 2. Assets in IRA (and Keogh) accounts were only about 4 percent as large as pension fund assets in 1981.[9] By 1989, accumulation of personal saving in IRA accounts amounted to $493.7 billion and was almost 27 percent as large as pension fund assets. Without the precipitous decline in IRA contributions after the 1986 bill, IRA assets apparently would have continued to grow.

At the individual level, the importance of IRAs for contributing house-

Security wealth is $83,700 and the median of pension wealth $11,200); the median of housing wealth is $38,000 and the median of liquid financial assets is only $10,000, for households with heads age 65 to 70.

[9] The data are reported in Piacentini and Cerino (1990) and include IRA and Keogh assets together. It is apparent, however, that in the later years the vast majority of the assets are in IRA accounts.

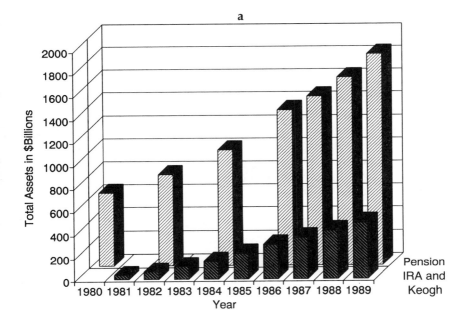

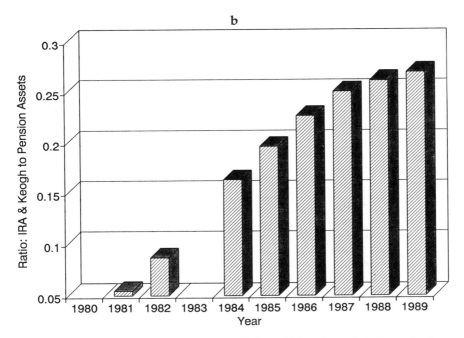

FIGURE 2. *Private pension versus IRA and Keogh.* **a.** *total assets;* **b.** *ratio of total assets.*

holds grew rapidly as well. The median ratio of IRA to other financial assets (excluding stocks and bonds) increased from essentially zero in 1980 to 0.75 in 1986, for households with accounts in 1986. If stocks and bonds are included, the ratio was 0.46. Most households without IRA saving in 1986 were essentially nonsavers, like the majority of American households. The median level of their financial assets was about $1,500 in 1986. As the following discussion will show, a large fraction of IRA savers also saved very little before the advent of the IRA program.

The realization that a large fraction of Americans do not save at all is important in assessing the impact of the IRA program. The data presented below suggest to us that IRA savers increased their total saving substantially after 1982. Many were saving very little before they began to contribute to an IRA. But many households did not save before and still do not. A significant proportion of these nonsavers will have low lifetime incomes and Social Security retirement benefits will replace a large fraction of their annual preretirement earnings. They may expect to maintain their preretirement standard of living with no personal saving and may never save through an IRA account.

But a large fraction of households with modest lifetime incomes would have been IRA savers under the pre-1986 legislation. The percent of households with IRA accounts in 1986 ranged from close to zero for young households with very low incomes to over 70 percent among older households with high incomes, as shown in Figure 3.[10] Like other saving, IRA saving increases with age and income. Over 50 percent of households with annual income above $20,000 would have opened an IRA account before they retired, based on the 1986 participation rate of households with heads 55 to 65 and income over $20,000. About 60 percent in this age bracket with incomes over $30,000 had accounts and 65 percent of those with incomes over $40,000.[11] Thus, relative to other saving, IRA saving is very widespread.

IRAs sometimes are portrayed as held by only a few and concentrated among the wealthy. About 60 percent of 1986 IRA accounts and 50 percent of IRA assets were held by households with incomes of less than $50,000.[12] Only 34 percent of non-IRA financial assets are held by house-

[10] Figure 3 is based on SIPP data. Over 80 percent of older high-income households contributed, according to SCF data.

[11] Based on SIPP data. Based on SCF data, 65 percent, 70 percent, and 77 percent, respectively, of households in this age group had accounts.

[12] Families with income less than $50,000 held 76 percent of the accounts and 66 percent of the balances, according to SIPP data. The family data corresponds more closely to an IRS tax unit than the household data.

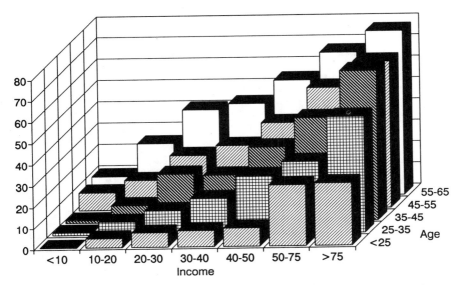

FIGURE 3. *Percent with IRA accounts, households, by income and age, 1986.*

holds with incomes less than $50,000.[13] Over one quarter of all households had accounts in 1986.[14] And, a large fraction of families that did not have accounts in 1986 would have had accounts before they retired. Thus, it may be more accurate to say that IRAs are widespread among potential savers.

II. IRA SAVING VERSUS OTHER SAVING: 1980 to 1989

If IRA saving substituted for other saving, one might have expected the proportion of persons saving in other forms to decline as the proportion saving through IRAs increased. Graphed in Figure 4 are the proportion of households contributing to an IRA in each year and the proportion of households with positive saving in non-IRA assets. (Figure 4a includes stocks and bonds and Figure 4b excludes stocks and bonds.) The graphs show that between 1980 and 1989 there was essentially no change in the proportion of households with non-IRA financial asset saving. The pro-

[13] Based on SCF data.

[14] 26.1 percent based on SIPP and 29.7 based on SCF.

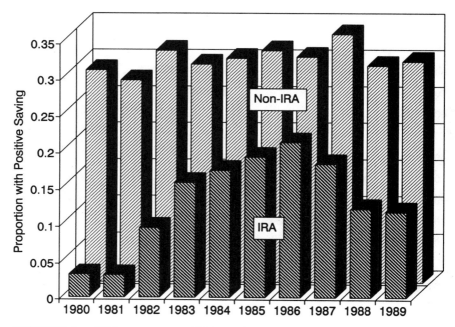

FIGURE 4a. *IRA versus non-IRA savings, 1980–1989. including stocks and bonds.*

portion making IRA contributions grew from 3 percent to 20 percent and then declined to 10 percent after the 1986 legislation.

Although we would expect the proportion of households with other saving to decline—if there were widespread substitution of IRA for other saving—it could be that even if IRA savers reduced other saving, most would still have some saving in other forms. In this case, the proportion with positive non-IRA saving would not change much. Thus we turn to consideration of the change in saving balances.

III. CHANGE IN IRA VERSUS NON-IRA ASSET BALANCES

In this section we consider whether the data appear consistent with the possibility that IRA contributions represented no addition to total saving, but only a reshuffling of existing asset balances or a switching of new saving from non-IRA to IRA accounts. The analysis is based on the changes in non-IRA financial asset balances as IRA balances increased.

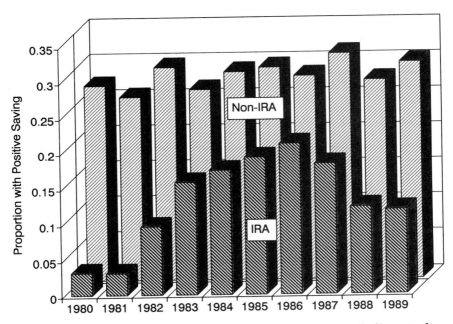

FIGURE 4b. *IRA versus non-IRA saving, 1980–1989, excluding stocks and bonds.*

In particular, we ask whether non-IRA balances declined, as the substitution (or reshuffling) hypothesis suggests. There are two ways that substitution could occur: one is that existing pre-1982 assets were transferred into IRAs in subsequent years. The other is that beginning in 1982 new saving was in the form of IRAs instead of non-IRA financial assets; IRA saving displaced non-IRA saving.

Three versions of the change in non-IRA balances are discussed. The first is based on the balances of respondents to successive Consumer Expenditure Surveys between 1980 and 1988. The second uses the same data but adjusts for the change in the attributes of contributor respondents to successive CES surveys. In both instances, the comparison is based on the balances of the random samples interviewed in successive surveys; the same respondents are not followed from year to year. The third version compares the balances of the same respondents interviewed through the Survey of Consumer Finances in 1983 and 1986. The goal is to judge whether the increase in IRA balances was accompanied by a transfer of assets from non-IRA accounts or by a reduction in new saving in non-IRA assets.

A. IRA versus Non-IRA Asset Balances: CES Data, 1980 to 1988

Each quarter the Consumer Expenditure Survey obtains information on a new random sample of households.[15] Thus, each survey represents a snapshot of households in that quarter. Data are obtained on income, assets, and other household characteristics. The average age of the head of the respondent households was about forty-six in each of our quarterly samples. We have combined data from the quarterly surveys to obtain annual averages.[16] These data are merged with IRA balances obtained from the SIPP (1985 to 1987).

The median IRA balance of contributors was about $1,700 in 1982.[17] By 1986 the median had increased to almost $8,000, and over one-quarter of households had IRA accounts. What happened to other financial asset balances over this time period?

Recall the two substitution possibilities: transfers and displacement of new saving. If IRA balances were accumulated by making repeated transfers from other accounts, the balances in other accounts should have declined as the IRA balances increased. If IRA saving displaced non-IRA saving after 1982, so that post-1982 respondents had begun to save in IRA accounts instead of in other accounts, the typical 1986 respondent with an IRA account should have had less money in other assets than the typical 1982 respondent. That is, even if no transfers were made from existing 1982 balances, if new saving by households after 1982 were in the form of IRAs instead of other assets, then the accumulated balance in other assets should have been lower for households surveyed in 1986 than for households surveyed in 1982. This is because the typical 1986 respondent would have accumulated less saving in other accounts in the previous four years than the typical 1982 respondent would have accumulated over the four years prior to 1982. For example, suppose that in 1982 the typical forty-six-year-old had been saving $2,000 per year in bank accounts for the past four years. That person would have accumulated $8,000 in bank accounts by 1982 (ignoring interest accumulation). If after 1982 IRA saving completely

---

[15] More precisely, a new panel is started each quarter and households in each panel are surveyed five times (each quarter) over the following fifteen months. Only households with heads 18 to 65 are included in this analysis and households with a self-employed member are excluded.

[16] All quarterly surveys conducted in a calendar year are included in the annual average for that year. This means, for example, that the percent of households making IRA contributions in a year will not match the IRS figure for the percentage of tax returns showing an IRA contribution for a tax year.

[17] The median contribution in 1982, based on CES data.

replaced other saving, the typical forty-six-year-old in 1986 would have saved $2,000 a year between 1983 and 1986 in an IRA but nothing in other accounts. The person who was forty-six years old in 1986 would have $8,000 in an IRA account but nothing in a regular bank account. IRA balances simply would have replaced other balances. Total assets of the 1986 forty-six-year-old would be the same as the total assets of the 1982 forty-six-year-old.

The data are shown in Figure 5. The figure shows that there was no systematic decline in the non-IRA balances of contributors as their IRA balances increased. These data show the assets of the typical household in different years, not the change over time for the same household. Thus, if there were no change in saving behavior, no change in returns on assets, and no change in household income, balances would be expected to be approximately the same over this time period. But nominal balances might be expected to rise as nominal income grows.

Figure 5a shows that by 1986, the median IRA balance was about the same as the median balance in other financial assets and was higher than pre-1982 balances in other financial assets (excluding stocks and bonds).

The total financial assets of 1982 respondent contributors (including IRAs but excluding stocks and bonds from other assets) was about $9,427.[18] A direct comparison with the total 1986 balance is not possible because the CES data do not provide the IRA balance. Thus the totals are not shown in the figures. But non-IRA asset balances based on SIPP data are essentially the same as the CES balances and the totals, including IRA balances, based on SIPP data should be close to the total assets of CES respondents. Based on this assumption, the total assets of 1986 contributor respondents were 90 percent greater than the total assets of 1982 contributor respondents, $17,900 versus $9,427. The increase between 1980 and 1986 was 248 percent.

Similar trends are revealed in Figure 5b, which includes stocks and bonds in non-IRA assets. The total financial assets of contributor respondents, including stocks and bonds, increased by 71 percent ($21,650 versus $12,660) between 1982 and 1986 and by 214 percent between 1980 and 1986.[19]

In summary, non-IRA assets of respondents to successive CES surveys did not decline as IRA assets increased between 1982 and 1986.

---

[18] Assuming that the 1982 household IRA balance was equal to the 1982 IRA contribution.

[19] The median asset balances appear to be unusually high in 1982 (see Figure 4a). On the other hand, the new 1982 contributors may have had asset levels that differed from those of earlier contributors, who did not have firm-provided pensions.

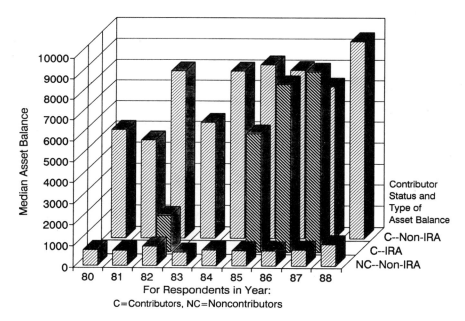

FIGURE 5a. *IRA versus non-IRA asset balances by IRA contributor, excluding stocks and bonds.*

Instead, non-IRA assets increased as well. Total assets of 1986 respondent contributors were much larger than the assets of respondents at the outset of or prior to the IRA program. It is apparent that IRA contributions were not funded by withdrawing funds from pre-1982 assets. Indeed, 1986 IRA balances were larger than pre-1982 non-IRA assets. It also seems apparent from the data that the typical IRA contributor was not accustomed to accumulating assets at an annual rate equal to the typical IRA contribution. In addition, the data suggest that the new IRA saving of contributors did not replace saving that otherwise would have gone into non-IRA assets. Assets in both forms were larger in 1986 than in 1982. Total assets were very much larger in 1986.

B. IRA versus Non-IRA Balances of Like Groups: CES Data, 1980 to 1988

In the preceding section, the assets of the typical contributor respondent in a year such as 1986 were compared to the assets of the typical contributor respondent in an earlier year such as 1982, at the outset of the IRA program. The respondents to each CES represent a random sample of the

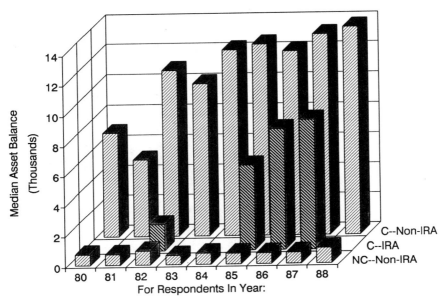

FIGURE 5b. *IRA versus non-IRA asset balances by IRA contributor, including stocks and bonds.*

population in that year. But the characteristics of families who were making IRA contributions may have changed over time. In particular, pre-1982 contributors did not have employer-provided pension plans and the non-IRA assets of these contributors may have differed from the assets of the much larger group that began to contribute after the 1982 legislation.

To correct for this ambiguity, we consider the non-IRA assets of more closely equivalent households. For example, instead of comparing the assets of the typical 1986 respondent contributor to the assets of the typical 1980 respondent contributor, we ask for the assets in 1980 of households that were "like" the households who made IRA contributions in 1986. In 1980 most of the like households were not eligible for an IRA. But by defining "like" groups, the 1980 and 1986 assets of "comparable" households can be compared. The groups are comparable except that the 1986 respondents had the opportunity to make IRA contributions for several years, while the 1980 respondents had not had the opportunity.

To identify groups of "contributor-like" households, 1985–1986 contributors are used to define the "contributor group." The 1985–1986 data are used to predict the probability that a household with given income

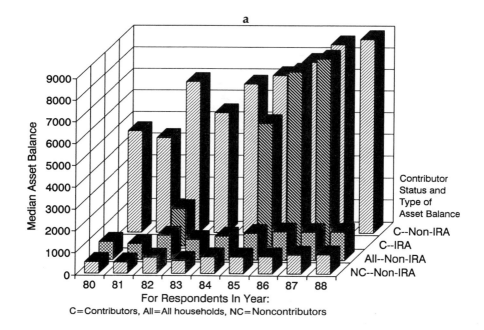

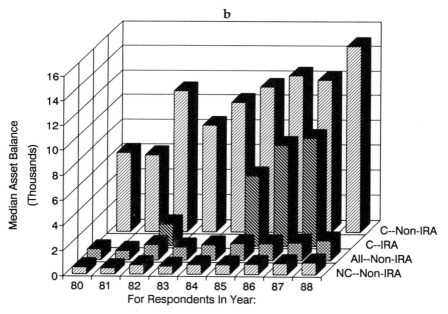

FIGURE 6. *IRA versus non-IRA balances for like groups.* **a.** *excluding stocks and bonds, 1980–1988;* **b.** *including stocks and bonds, 1980–1988.*

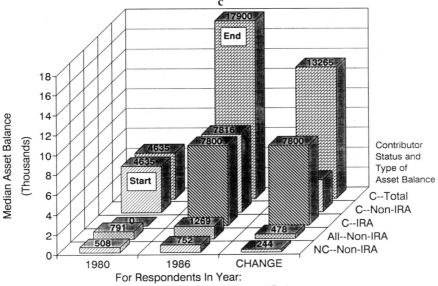

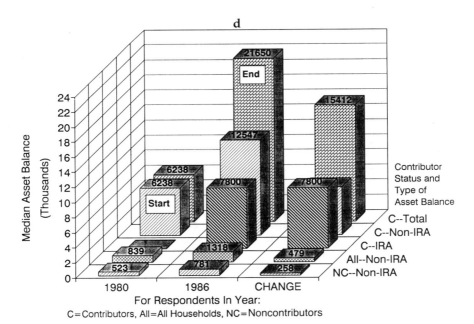

FIGURE 6. *IRA versus non-IRA balances for like groups.* **c.** *excluding stocks and bonds, 1980–1986;* **d.** *including stocks and bonds, 1980–1986.*

and age of head contributes to an IRA account. For example, about 68 percent of households with heads aged fifty-five to sixty-five and income over $50,000 contributed to an IRA account; about 45 percent of those aged forty-five to fifty-five with incomes between $30,000 and $50,000 contributed. Based on the 1985–1986 proportions, 68% of the 1980 households in the fifty-five to sixty-five age range with income over $50,000 are randomly assigned to the "contributor-like" group, and so forth for other groups. In practice the probabilities are calculated for sixteen age-income categories. An adjustment is then made for the "individual saving effect" reflected in the higher non-IRA assets of persons within each group who have IRAs.[20]

Comparisons similar to those in the previous section can now be made. They are shown in Figures 6a and 6b for the years 1980 through 1988 and in Figures 6c and 6d for 1980 and 1986 only. The conclusions are much the same as those based on the unadjusted data, graphed in Figures 5a and 5b.

It is easiest to consider first the comparison between 1980 and 1986, shown in Figures 6c and 6d. These figures also show total assets of contributors, including IRA and non-IRA amounts. The data are summarized in Table 1. The 1980 IRA balance of contributor-like respondent households was close to zero. By 1986 the median had increased to $7,800. Contributor-like 1980 respondents had a median of $4,635 in non-IRA financial assets, as shown in Figure 6c (excluding stocks and bonds). The 1986 respondents had a median of $7,816 in non-IRA assets, an increase of 69 percent.[21] In addition to the increase in non-IRA assets, the 1986 contributors had an additional $7,800 in IRA assets. Total financial assets of contributor-like respondents increased from about $4,635 in

[20] The adjustment is based on the difference between the non-IRA assets of an actual contributor and the assets of a randomly predicted contributor in the same age and income cell. It is the ratio of the median assets of observed contributors to the median of predicted contributors within each of the 1985–1986 age-income cells. Non-IRA assets of the like group in other years are obtained by first using the contributor probabilities described in the text to identify the like group, then calculating actual non-IRA assets for this group, and then applying the adjustment ratio. Separate calculations are made for the contributor and noncontributor groups. Income is converted to 1986 dollars using the income growth observed in the CESs.

[21] In years for which the assets of "contributor-like" respondents can be compared to the assets of actual contributors the correspondence is typically close. For example, the median non-IRA assets (excluding stocks and bonds) of actual 1983 respondents was $5,500; the predicted assets of "contributor-like" respondents was $5,472. The implication we draw is that the correspondence would also be close for 1980, for example, when the correspondence cannot be seen because then there were few contributors. It also means that the

TABLE 1.
CES-SIPP Summary.

Contributor status and asset	Respondents in		% Change
	1980	1986	
	Excluding stocks and bonds		
Contributor-like:			
Non-IRA assets	4635	7816	68.6
IRA assets	0	7800	—
Total assets	4635	17900	286.2
Noncontributor-like:			
Total assets	508	752	48.0
	Including stocks and bonds		
Contributor-like:			
Non-IRA assets	6238	12547	101.1
IRA assets	0	7800	—
Total assets	6238	21650	247.1
Noncontributor-like:			
Total assets	523	781	49.3

The 1986 IRA and total asset balances are from SIPP. Median 1986 non-IRA assets based on the CES and the SIPP are virtually the same ($8,050 versus $8,040 excluding and $11,500 versus $12,200 including stocks and bonds).

1980 to about $17,900 in 1986, an increase of 286 percent.[22] Comparable data are shown in Figure 6d, with stocks and bonds included in non-IRA financial assets. In this case, the increase in total assets between 1980 and 1986 was 247 percent.

---

conclusions using 1986 as a base would have been essentially the same if 1983 had been used as a base. For example, if 1983 was used as the base, the natural comparison would have been to ask if 1986 "contributor-like" respondents saved less in non-IRA assets than would have been predicted based on the distribution of assets of contributors by age and income in 1983. The answer would be no; they saved about the same, plus they accumulated a substantial balance in IRA accounts.

[22] Again, based on the match between SIPP and CES median asset balances in 1986, as discussed in the previous section.

TABLE 2.
Time and Saving Deposit Rates in Commercial Banks.

Ending in	Average over the preceding			
	three years	four years	five years	six years
1980	7.53	7.02	6.72	6.59
1982	10.28	9.58	8.87	8.31
1983	10.07	9.82	9.35	8.80
1986	7.84	7.99	8.48	8.95

Is it likely that without the IRA program the assets of like households would have nearly tripled over this period? There are at least two reasons why non-IRA assets might have increased. One is that nominal income increased and nominal saving might have increased as well. The other is that changes in the rate of return on financial assets may have changed. The increase in median income between 1980 and 1986 was 48 percent, much less than the increase in total financial assets: 286 percent excluding and 247 percent including stocks and bonds. Indeed the income increase was less than the increase in non-IRA assets: 69.6 percent excluding stocks and bonds and 101.1 percent including stocks and bonds. Assets may also have increased because of capital gains in the stock market.[23] But the financial assets of most savers are not in stocks. Indeed, the increase in non-IRA assets excluding stocks and bonds was not much greater than the increase when they are included, suggesting that stock market capital gains is not the explanation.

It may be that non-IRA balances should be considered relative to the overall increase in financial assets for all respondents. The trend in financial assets for the non-contributor-like group is also shown in the figures. The increase between 1980 and 1986 was 48 percent, much less than the percent increase for contributors.

What about the return on commercial bank accounts, where the bulk of most households' financial assets are held? Average time and saving deposit rates in commercial banks in the years preceding 1980, 1982, 1983, and 1986 are shown in Table 2.[24] The data for 1983 are included in anticipation of the same issue that will be raised with respect to the data in the next section.

---

[23] The Standard and Poor stock market index more than doubled between 1982 and 1986. The expected increase in financial asset balances would be much less than this because only a small proportion of asset holders have significant equity in the stock market.

[24] The rates are from the *Savings Institutions Sourcebook,* U.S. League of Savings Institutions.

The rate of return in the years preceding 1986 was somewhat higher than the rate in the years preceding 1980, but the differences are not large enough to explain the large increase in financial assets. Even the increase in non-IRA financial assets seems large relative to the increase that might have been expected based on 1980 non-IRA assets.

Based on these data, it seems to us very unlikely that IRA replaced non-IRA saving; that there was no gain in net saving. Again, it is apparent from the low 1980 asset balances of contributor-like households ($4,635) that before the advent of IRAs the typical contributor-like household had not been accumulating financial assets at an annual rate close to an IRA contribution, typically $2,000 or $4,000 in 1986. (The mean was $2,308.) It is also clear that the increase in IRA balances was not funded by withdrawing funds from pre-1982 balances, which were substantially smaller than the $7,800 put into IRA accounts.

Data for these two years, including stocks and bonds, are shown in Figure 6d. The data for all years from 1980 to 1988 (Figures 6a and 6b) reveal the same trends as the two-year comparison.

The adjusted CES data discussed in this section provide an informal picture very comparable to the results of the formal analysis in Venti and Wise (1990a), which also was based on these same CES data. Indeed a general test of the behavioral validity of the model used in that analysis was to predict the saving behavior of households in the pre-IRA period, using model estimates based on post-1982 data. In effect, with reference to Figure 6, the model predicted quite accurately the low non-IRA saving in 1980, based on estimates in later years when total saving (including IRA and non-IRA saving) was much higher. That is, the model predicted well what saving would be if the IRA limit was set to zero.

C. IRA versus Non-IRA Balances: SCF Data, 1983 to 1986

The discussion in the previous section is based on the comparison of the asset balances of the different respondents to successive surveys, before and after the general availability of IRAs. In that case, asset balances may have increased during the time between the surveys because of income growth, but age did not change systematically (the average age was about forty-six in each year). An alternative to comparing different household samples in different years is to compare the balances of the same households over time. In this case, asset balances may increase as the households age, and possibly as their incomes grow as well.

Such a comparison can be made using the 1983 and 1986 SCF data. We begin with respondents to the 1986 survey. Only households aged twenty-four to sixty-five are included in the analysis and households with self-employed members are excluded. Non-IRA and IRA median

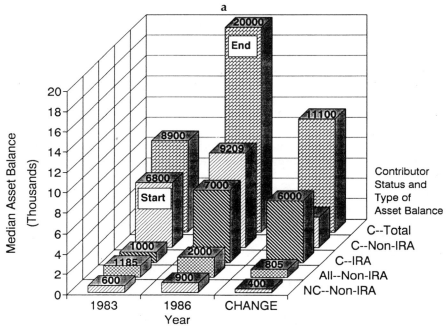

FIGURE 7a. *IRA versus non-IRA balances, SCF 1986 respondents, excluding stocks and bonds.*

balances for this group in 1983 and 1986 and the change in balances between these years by 1986 IRA contributor status are shown in Figure 7. Stocks and bonds are excluded from Figure 7a and included in Figure 7b. These figures also include total assets of contributors, including both IRA and non-IRA balances, and show the change in assets between 1983 and 1986. The data are reproduced in Table 3. Again, the non-IRA assets of contributors did not decline as IRA assets increased between 1983 and 1986; on the contrary, they increased substantially. The median 1983 non-IRA asset balance (excluding stocks and bonds) of households with IRA accounts in 1986 was $6,360. Clearly, prior to 1983, this group had not been accumulating assets at the rate of the typical IRA contribution. And clearly the $6,000 increase in IRA balances (from $1,000 in 1983 to $7,000 in 1986) was not funded by transferring funds from the 1983 balance ($6,360) in non-IRA accounts.

Without the IRA program, what increase in this 1983 non-IRA asset balance would be expected over the next three years? In fact, the ob-

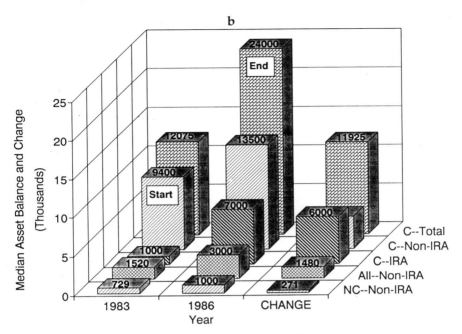

b

FIGURE 7b. *IRA versus non-IRA balances, SCF 1986 respondents, including stocks and bonds.*

served 44.8 percent increase was equivalent to an annual growth rate of over 13 percent. The increase in all assets combined, including IRAs, was much greater than this. IRA assets also grew, by $6,000. The median of total assets more than doubled, increasing by $11,100 from $8,900 to $20,000.

Without IRA contributions, would the 1983 balance of $6,360 have been expected to increase by almost threefold, to $20,000, by 1986? As discussed in the previous section, the increase in total assets may be determined in part by income growth and the increase in age, and the data could be confounded by differences in economic trends prior to the two dates, that is, differences in rates of return. The increase in non-IRA assets between 1983 and 1986 is apparently not the result of the growth in stock values over this period. The percentage increase in non-IRA assets was about the same when stocks and bonds were excluded as when they were included.

Assets may have been expected to increase with age and income. We have controlled for these effects by predicting 1986 assets based on the

TABLE 3.
SCF Summary.

Contributor status and asset	Year		% Change
	1983	1986	
Excluding stocks and bonds			
Contributors in 1986:			
Non-IRA assets	6360	9209	44.8
IRA assets	1000	7000	600.0
Total assets	8900	20000	125.7
Non-Contributors:			
Total assets	600	900	50.0
Including stocks and bonds			
Contributors in 1986:			
Non-IRA assets	9400	13500	43.6
IRA assets	1000	7000	600.0
Total assets	12075	24000	98.8
Non-Contributors			
Total assets	729	1000	37.2

distribution of contributor assets by age and income in 1983. Adjusting for the three-year age increase and the income increase between 1983 and 1986, the balance would have been expected to increase by about 25 percent, excluding stocks and bonds, and about 31 percent including stocks and bonds. Including IRA contributions the actual increase was almost 126 percent excluding stocks and bonds and almost 100 percent including stocks and bonds. Commercial bank rates in the years preceding 1986 were lower than the rates preceding 1983, as shown in the previous section. The asset growth cannot be explained by unusually high rates of return.

Thus, judging from the SCF data, it seems to us unlikely that the IRA contributions simply substituted for saving that would have occurred anyway. In particular, that inference seems implausible based on the information available in 1983. And again, based on the 1983 balance of $6,360 the 1986 contributors prior to 1983 had not been accustomed to saving nearly as much as they saved over the next three years. Comparison of the SCF with the CES summary tabulation in the previous section shows that the two data sets yield essentially the same implications.

TABLE 4.
Change in Non-IRA Saving when IRA Contributor Status Changes Bank Accounts.

	1985 Noncontributor	1985 Contributor
1984 Noncontributor	−64.6 (61.4)	−377.4 (248.7)
1984 Contributor	148.6 (317.0)	−470.3 (182.7)
F = 2.565		

IV. CHANGE IN OTHER SAVING WITH CHANGE IN IRA STATUS

If non-IRA saving is reduced when IRA saving is increased, then when a household that was not contributing begins to add to an IRA, that household should reduce non-IRA saving. Likewise, when a household that was contributing stops, non-IRA saving should increase. The SIPP panel data allow calculation of the change in non-IRA saving when IRA contributor status changes. This simple calculation controls directly for changes in saving behavior across families because it is based on changes over time for the same families.[25]

Table 4 shows that there is a small reduction ($377.4) in non-IRA bank account financial asset saving for new contributors and a small increase ($148.6) for households that stop contributing. But the changes are only a small fraction of the typical IRA contribution, about $2,300.

Estimates incorporating all non-IRA financial assets—bank accounts, bonds, and stocks—are shown in Table 5. These data also reveal that the change in non-IRA saving is much less than the typical IRA contribution. Although these data suggest some substitution, none of the estimates is statistically significant. In particular, the hypothesis that there is no change in non-IRA saving with change in IRA contributor status cannot be rejected (as indicated by the F-statistics).

V. CHANGE IN SAVING BEHAVIOR AND THE COINCIDENCE HYPOTHESIS

The data in the previous section suggest that the IRA program induced substantial new saving. There is, however, one possible, although we

---

[25] The calculations and the data set are explained in detail in Venti and Wise (1990b).

TABLE 5.
Change in Non-IRA Saving when IRA Contributor Status Changes Bank Accounts, Bonds, and Stocks.

	1985 Noncontributor	1985 Contributor
1984 *Noncontributor*	89.4 (102.1)	−193.5 (413.6)
1984 *Contributor*	630.3 (527.2)	186.2 (303.9)
F = 2.565		

believe improbable, alternative scenario that could explain the dramatic increase in the financial assets of contributors: A sudden change in the saving behavior of IRA contributors that just happened to coincide with the introduction of IRAs. Change in behavior must be distinguished from change in saving and from the confounding influence of person-specific saving behavior. All of the data presented earlier rely on the change in saving over time—for the same or for "like" households—to infer whether IRAs replaced non-IRA saving. The SIPP data in the previous section show that non-IRA saving did not decrease much when households who were not previously contributing to an IRA began to make contributions. Consideration of the change in non-IRA saving when IRA contributor status changes controls explicitly for "individual-specific" saving behavior. Some households are "savers," they save more than the typical household in all forms. Thus, the answer to the question, "Do IRA contributors have less non-IRA saving than non-contributors?," is no, they have more assets in both forms. This could be because IRAs do not substitute for other saving. But it could also reflect the fact that IRA contributors are savers and, in the absence of the IRA option, they would save even more in other forms.[26] This "individual-specific" saving effect is dealt with by considering the change in non-IRA saving of a household when the IRA saving of that same household changes. If non-IRA saving of a household increased when IRA saving increased, for example, this could not be attributed to the generally high saving propensity of IRA

[26] This affect may make it difficult to draw conclusions from the comparison of IRA contributors and noncontributors at a point in time. Thus some commentators have resolved that no reliable inferences can be drawn from cross-section data, that is, pertaining to a sample of households for a single year. But all of the studies by Venti and Wise, (1986, 1987, 1988, 1990a, 1990b, 1991a, 1991b), for example, and the study by Gale and Scholz (1990), although based on cross-section data (or a series of independent cross sections) consider changes in asset balances to measure saving and use accumulated asset balances—given age and income and other personal attributes—to control for individual-specific saving behavior.

contributors. Using the SCF data, the issue is controlled for by considering the change in the non-IRA and IRA assets of the same households between 1983 and 1986. With respect to the CES data, individual-specific saving effects are controlled for by comparing random samples of "contributor-like" households in 1980 with "contributor-like" households in subsequent years. Thus the data are not confounded by comparing savers with nonsavers; the comparison pertains only to savers. The results from each of the three data sources control for the higher propensity of some households to save, in all forms.

But the results do not control for possible changes in saving behavior. Nonsavers could suddenly become savers or low savers could suddenly start to save more. This possibility cannot be addressed directly with either the SIPP or the SCF data but can be addressed with the CES data. With respect to the SIPP data, were the households that changed from non-IRA to IRA contributor status on the verge of changing their saving behavior, independent of the IRA program? Would they have increased their saving even without the IRA option? Was it that they did not reduce non-IRA saving when they contributed $2,300 to an IRA account because they were going to increase total saving by $2,300 anyway and the IRA was a convenient way to do it? This seems to us to be a possible but improbable coincidental explanation of the increase in saving.

With respect to the SCF data: Were the 1986 IRA contributors the households whose saving behavior—for reasons not apparent in 1983—was about to change dramatically over the next three years, independent of the new IRA option? Did the change in saving behavior just happen to coincide with the advent of the IRA? On its face, this possibility seems an improbable explanation. The dramatic increase in asset balances cannot be explained by a sudden increase in income. The median increase in income for 1986 contributors was only 15.7 percent over the entire period, from 1983 to 1986.

The same question may be posed with respect to the CES data. In this case, more formal testing provides evidence against the hypothesis. Were households with IRA accounts in 1986 those that in 1982 were about to change their saving behavior dramatically? And, did this unexpected change—based on past saving behavior—just happen to coincide with the advent of the IRA program? Based on the CES data, IRA "contributor-like" households had $4,635 in non-IRA assets in 1980. By 1986, such households had a median of $17,900, including IRA assets. Were these households on the verge of an abrupt change in saving behavior that was destined to lead to a three-fold increase in financial assets over the next four or five years? As with the SIPP and the SCF data, there is no evidence to support this possibility and such a coincidence seems to us to be an improbable explanation for the change in financial asset balances.

But with respect to these data, the test reported in Venti and Wise (1990a) provides a more formal rejection of the coincidence hypothesis. Unlike the SCF data that pertain to the same households in 1983 and in 1986, the CES data pertain to random samples of similar households. For example, the 1980 survey respondents were about the same age as the 1986 respondents. If the saving behavior of contributors changed just as the IRA program was introduced, estimates of saving behavior based on post-1982 data should predict pre-1982 saving behavior poorly. But the formal model estimated on post-1982 data predicts well the pattern of saving by income in the absence of the IRA program, prior to 1982. If saving behavior had changed dramatically over this time period, one would expect a poor match between actual and predicted pre-1982 saving.

Because large-scale substitution of IRA for non-IRA saving is not found in the data, we have been drawn to consider a possible scenario in which the data might not reveal substitution that in fact occurred. But it is also possible that promotion of the IRA program spurred households to save more in other forms as well, which is consistent with the large increase in non-IRA saving as IRA assets began to accumulate. Or, the consideration of retirement needs concomitant with opening and funding an IRA may have induced more saving in other forms as well. Both the CES and the SCF data are consistent with the possibility that non-IRA—as well as IRA—saving increased after IRA contributions began. This possibility is consistent with evidence on the relationship between personal saving and firm pension plan saving, reviewed in Shefrin and Thaler (1988).

VI. LIMITATIONS OF THE THEORY

Many expressed views on the saving effects of IRAs are not based on empirical evidence but are speculations based on simple theoretical reasoning (see Gravelle 1989, 1991 for an extreme view). In some important respects, however, the empirical evidence is inconsistent with the predictions and the assumption embedded in the "theory-based" speculations. Although these models may provide some insight into how people should behave in a narrow financial sense, the predictions offer a poor description of how the public actually responded to the IRA program. Indeed, the assumptions are inconsistent with basic facts about IRA contributors and IRA saving. Moreover, the assumptions underlying the speculations virtually preclude any saving effect of IRAs. A more complete model must recognize the broader economic and psychological channels through which an aggressively promoted tax-advantaged savings plan may stimulate saving. Thus having presented the data, we emphasize the limitations of judgments based on restrictive assumptions about saving behavior that are embedded in the simple economic model. In our view it is important to determine from the data which assumptions are most consistent with the saving decisions of real people.

A. The Simple Model

The theoretical model underlying several recent judgments is what Burman, Cordes, and Ozanne (1990) call the "traditional approach" and what Gravelle (1989, 1991) calls the "conventional view." In this model, there is only one form of saving. Thus the assumption is that households treat IRA saving and other saving as perfectly fungible. Except for the tax advantage, a dollar saved in an IRA is no different than a dollar saved in another form. And, the "tax-price" difference is the only means by which the IRA program is permitted to affect individual behavior; IRAs simply provide a higher return on the one and only form of saving.

From this characterization of saving behavior, it is a short stride to the conclusion that IRAs will not stimulate saving. Burman, Cordes, and Ozanne (1990:266) state the case: "If saving is motivated by life-cycle consumption choices, two conditions must be satisfied if IRAs are to stimulate private saving. IRAs must change the after-tax return to the additional dollar saved for a significant number of savers and private saving must respond to such changes. The task is then to determine whether both of these conditions are likely to be met." Of course, if one assumes that IRAs and other saving are perfect substitutes, that only the marginal after-tax return matters, and that IRA savers were saving above the IRA limit, then there will be no change in the after-tax return on the next dollar saved and no change in saving. Furthermore, because the general consensus is that saving is not very responsive to the after-tax return, the boost to saving will be negligible even among those who were not saving above the IRA limit prior to the IRA program. Thus, following this simple model, the case against the saving effectiveness of IRAs can be closed without looking at the data.

More generally, there are four assumptions embedded in the simple theoretical framework that has been used by some to evaluate the saving effects of IRAs: The first is that most IRA contributors were already saving more than the IRA limit prior to the advent of the IRA program. (A related assumption is that the typical IRA saver had large accumulated financial asset balances that could be transferred easily to an IRA account.) The second is that the program inducement to save operates entirely through the after-tax rate of return. The IRA tax advantage encourages saving by increasing the return on saving, up to the IRA limit. But a household that is already saving more than the limit does not benefit from the higher rate of return on an additional dollar saved. The third, and most important assumption, is that IRA saving and other forms of saving are treated by real people as perfect substitutes. The fourth, and related to the third, is that the promotion of IRA saving had no effect on their use.

B. The Evidence

We will consider these assumptions in turn, although it is not always possible to neatly separate them. In particular, it is not always clear whether an example should be thought of as contradicting the perfect substitutes assumption or the assumption that only the rate of return matters. Nonetheless, we have found it convenient to separate them in the discussion. The simple model does not explain several prominent features of IRA saving, let alone their saving effects, a much more complicated issue.

1. Contributors Were Saving More than the IRA Limit.   From the data discussed previously, it seems apparent that the typical IRA contributor, prior to the advent of the IRA program, had not been saving nearly as much as the typical IRA contribution. Nor did the typical contributor fund IRA contributions by drawing down pre-1982, non-IRA financial asset balances. Both the CES and the SCF summary tabulations and Figures 6c and 7a, for example, show this clearly.

2. Only the After-Tax Rate of Return Matters.   Much of IRA saving behavior is inconsistent with saving decisions based solely on the rate of return. First, if only the rate of return is considered, strictly financial calculations show no difference between a "front-loaded" IRA—with an up-front tax deduction but payment of tax on withdrawal from the IRA account—and the "back-loaded" version—with payment of taxes on the contribution but no tax payment when the funds are withdrawn (if tax rates do not change). But the evidence is that real people prefer the up-front deduction. The here and now tax saving takes precedence over the long-term equivalence calculation. The United Kingdom experience with the Personal Equity Plan (PEP) provides evidence of the difference as viewed by savers. The U.K. plan is patterned after the U.S. IRA, but contributions are made on an after-tax basis, with no taxes paid when funds are withdrawn. Unlike the U.S. experience, financial institutions have found it difficult to attract contributions to the U.K. plan.

Second, the narrow rate of return analysis suggests that consumers can benefit by using tax-deductible borrowing (home equity loans in particular) to finance IRA contributions (Kotlikoff, 1990). The empirical evidence suggests, however, that this effect is either nonexistent or very small (Manchester and Poterba, 1989; Skinner, 1991; Venti and Wise 1991b).

Third, after the Tax Reform Act of 1986, households that were no longer eligible for the up-front tax deduction could still benefit from tax free compounding of the return. The dramatic drop in IRA contributions following the reform is inconsistent with saving decisions based strictly on the rate of return. This drop can be explained neither by changes in eligibility nor changes in marginal tax rates (Long, 1990). Instead, the response suggests that the up-front deduction is important. It is apparently what gets the attention of people.

3. People Treat IRA and Other Saving As Perfect Substitutes.   To begin, consider the implications of these three assumptions: (1) IRA contributors would save more than the IRA limit in the absence of the IRA option, (2) only the after-tax rate of return matters, and (3) real people treat IRA and other saving as perfect substitutes. Based on these assumptions, the introduction of IRAs may even reduce saving. The reasoning is that if saving is subsidized, by reducing the consumption that must be given up today to save for tomorrow, a saver can give up less today and still have the same income to spend tomorrow. (A "target saver," for example, could save less today and still reach target asset accumulation at retirement.) Thus even less may be saved today. But this reasoning breaks down if all forms of saving are not perfect substitutes in the minds of the real people who make saving decisions.

Consider this example: I devote 2 percent of my earnings to a bank saving account and 98 percent to other things. A new subsidized saving vehicle is introduced—there is a sale on this type of saving—and it is heavily promoted as a means of assuring my financial well-being after retirement. If the old and the new types of saving are perfect substitutes, and the promotion has no effect on saving, new saving is likely to be financed by reducing old bank account saving. But if savers view the two types of vehicles as different accounts, like the mental accounts suggested by Shefrin and Thaler (1988) and Thaler (1990), for example, new saving may be financed by reducing the 98 percent of income devoted to other things rather than by reducing the 2 percent of income devoted to bank account saving. The standard marginal arguments do not hold if people think of the two forms of saving as different. This could be true even without the promotion; it would be more pronounced to the extent that the promotion is effective, as discussed later. Thus even people who would otherwise save more than the IRA limit may increase their total saving with the "sale on IRA saving."

There are obvious reasons why IRAs and other saving are not perfect substitutes in theory. In particular, there is a penalty on withdrawal of IRA assets before age 59.5. They are less liquid. Thus persons who want to save for the short run may not want to use the IRA mechanism.[27] But, more important, what is the empirical evidence on substitutability?

Data for persons over 59.5 demonstrate the limitation of the perfect substitutes assumption. Persons over age 59.5 are able to take IRA deductions but do not face any penalty for withdrawal of IRA funds. In terms of availability and liquidity, IRAs for this age group are barely distinguishable from other forms of saving. The one difference is the higher after-tax rate of return available through the IRA account, apparently making the IRA unambiguously "better" than a conventional saving account. Yet even most persons over 59.5 do not have IRA accounts. The empirical fact is at odds with the implication of the perfect substitutability assumption, suggesting that there is more to the IRA program than the simple "tax-price" subsidy of a simple form of saving, the characterization at the heart of the simple model.

More general data for all age groups also reject the extreme perfect substitutes view. If all forms of saving were perfect substitutes, all savers would save first in the IRA form and only save in other forms if they saved more than the IRA limit. But a large fraction of persons that do not make IRA contributions save in other forms.

Another empirical regularity also suggests that the traditional model mischaracterizes the IRA as a perfect substitute for other saving. IRA contributions, unlike other saving, are bunched in the month preceding the filing of tax returns. If the distinction between IRAs and other saving is solely the tax advantage, then investors should open these accounts some fifteen months earlier to take advantage of the higher return on IRA accounts. That they do not behave this way suggests a behavioral motivation other than or in addition to the rate of return.

4. *The Promotion of IRAs Had No Effect on Their Use.* Different modes of saving may be treated by real people as distinct goods for several reasons. Whatever these reasons may be, to the extent that the promotion of IRAs is successful, the promotion may magnify the distinctions among modes of saving and indeed may help to create them. The greater

---

[27] The studies by Joines and Manegold (1991) and Gale and Scholz (1990) relax the perfect substitutability assumption by explicitly incorporating the withdrawal penalty in a three-period theoretical model. Their theoretical predictions of the saving effects of IRAs are ambiguous.

the promotional success, the more IRA saving may be distinguished by savers from other forms of saving. In particular the widespread promotion that accompanied the IRA program in the 1982 to 1986 period may have served in part to distinguish IRA saving from other forms. The simple theory leaves no role for the effect of advertising and other forms of promotion on IRA saving.

Although it is difficult to assess quantitatively the psychological and informational role played by the promotion, the direction of the effect seems clear. The IRA fanfare psychologically earmarked IRAs for retirement, possibly tending to limit the substitutability of IRAs for funds saved in other "mental accounts." A goal of the promotion was to make families more aware of the need to adequately save for retirement. Many may have concluded that a special account for retirement saving was a good way to foster behavior to which they would not otherwise have adhered. The "sale" on this type of saving, of course, made the idea especially appealing. Indeed the illiquidity of IRAs may be considered an advantage by many; it may help to ensure behavior that would not otherwise be followed. It may be a means of self-control. Thought of in this way, IRA saving may have promoted greater saving in other forms as well. The effect may be similar to the "recognition effect" advanced by Cagan (1965) to explain the empirical finding that pension coverage was associated with higher levels of saving (see also Katona, 1965). Thus the promotion of saving accounts dedicated to particular uses may both limit substitution between accounts and increase investor awareness of the need to save for specific goals.

Several aspects of the public response to IRAs in the 1982 to 1986 period suggest to us that the fanfare accompanying IRAs was an important ingredient of their success. First, the bunching of IRA contributions during the media blitz preceding April 15 each year suggests that contributors are responsive to promotion. As Summers (1986) noted, IRAs, much like insurance, may be sold, not bought. Apparently the public was an easy sell at tax time. For a typical taxpayer, the last minute choice between writing a $800 check to the IRS or opening a $2,000 IRA may have been too alluring to pass up.

A second indication of the role of promotion is provided by Feenberg and Skinner (1989) who found that a large number of households were "falsely constrained"; they contributed exactly $2,000 when they were eligible to contribute more. Although transaction costs associated with opening a spousal account provide one explanation for this behavior, it is likely that the promotion, in which the amount $2,000 figured prominently, played a key role.

Third, investor behavior following the Tax Reform Act of 1986 provides an indication of promotional effects. As emphasized earlier, IRA contributions fell by much more than would be predicted given the changes in eligibility rules. This "overreaction" is at least in part attributable to widespread misunderstanding of the legislation (often reported at the time to have eliminated IRAs) and to the marked decline in the promotion of IRAs. Indeed, a recent survey revealed that about half of all persons eligible for an IRA deduction following the 1986 legislation mistakenly believed they were no longer eligible (*IRA Reporter*, 1988).

The emphasis here on the promotion and the "psychology of saving" that it may have engendered does not mean that the tax-advantage was unimportant. Surely it was critical to the success of the program. It seems apparent, however, that the promotion and fanfare played a critical role in parlaying the tax break into IRA contributions. The simple economic models that do not recognize this are likely to be blinded to an important explanation of the public response. Thus it seems to us that a complete understanding of the effects of the IRA program must capture substantially more than the limited reasoning embodied in the simple model.

C. What Makes IRAs Different?

If individuals behave as if all forms of saving are not perfect substitutes, what fosters the behavioral distinctions? We believe that the advertising plays a role. But any answer to this question is speculative. Although the simple model is at odds with prominent features of IRA saving and, in particular, the perfect substitutes assumption cannot be supported by the data, the source of the distinction among different forms of saving is not as clear. A possible explanation is provided by individual motives for saving and possibly the "psychology of saving."

Personal motives for saving suggest compartmentalization. If IRAs are held for different purposes than conventional accounts, then substitution possibilities may be limited from the perspective of many savers. For instance, assets accumulated for short-term goals such as a down payment on a home or a child's education may be unaffected by the introduction of an IRA promoting saving for retirement. How much of conventional saving is closely related to IRA saving? Stated reasons for saving may provide a rough indication. Avery et al. (1986) tabulated responses to the following question from the 1983 Survey of Consumer Finances: "People have different reasons for saving. What are your (family's) most important reasons for saving? Anything else?" Results are summarized by age and income in Table 6. At all income levels the precautionary motive ("emergencies") dominates retirement as a motive for saving. And only at ages above 55 does retirement dominate "emergencies." Even in this age group only half say they are saving for retire-

TABLE 6.

Purposes of Saving, Families with Head in Labor Force, by Family Income and Age of Head (percent of families in each group mentioning purpose).

	Purpose						
	Emergencies	Retirement	Education	Purchase home	Purchase durables	Travel	Expenses
Family income							
< $10,000	49.5	10.5	20.7	6.9	18.4	6.9	12.7
$10,000–19,999	53.8	18.0	16.0	10.2	15.7	10.9	7.3
$20,000–29,999	58.6	22.5	16.3	10.8	13.8	11.2	5.3
$30,000–49,999	48.8	30.9	21.7	8.8	14.3	11.4	5.1
$50,000 or more	50.9	37.8	23.4	4.3	11.1	10.8	4.9
Age of head							
Less than 25	52.5	4.9	16.2	16.1	24.2	12.0	10.2
25–34	55.6	8.8	18.6	15.3	18.5	8.9	7.2
35–44	55.4	20.7	26.4	7.6	13.9	12.6	5.4
45–54	52.4	35.9	18.2	3.1	11.5	10.0	5.2
55–64	44.5	52.0	11.1	1.9	8.2	10.9	7.3
65 and over	39.6	44.3	9.8	*	7.2	5.3	12.7

Source: Avery, Elliehausen, and Gustafson, 1986.

ment. Although such evidence is only suggestive, it indicates that much of non-IRA saving may be viewed as an imperfect substitute for IRA saving, which is narrowly targeted for retirement.

Further evidence on motives for saving is provided by the asset holdings of families on the eve of retirement. The data in Figure 1 suggest that the typical family saves little for retirement in the form of financial assets. For example, the median household financial asset balance including stock and bonds was $6,600 in 1984 for households with head age fifty-five to sixty-five. The family median is less than $3,700 (Venti and Wise, 1991b). Thus it appears that, for most families, the level of non-IRA financial asset saving destined to finance consumption in retirement is low. For the typical family it is thus unlikely that a new IRA contribution would substitute for funds that were previously targeted for retirement.

Shefrin and Thaler (1988) and Thaler (1990) have addressed these and other empirical regularities that they find inconsistent with the traditional life-cycle theory of saving. They argue that some of the limitations of the traditional theory can be overcome by modifications making the model more behaviorally realistic. One of their suggestions is to recognize that all forms of saving are not treated as fungible; individuals may have a system of "mental accounts" in which they save for various purposes. Some of these accounts may, by choice, be easily spent (e.g. checking). As a means of precommitment or self-control other accounts may be viewed as inaccessible. Shefrin and Thaler place pensions in the latter category. Apparently an IRA also would be viewed as inaccessible, according to their view. For many individuals the ability to place some saving "off-limits" may actually be a desirable attribute. To the extent that "mental accounts" reflect individual saving behavior, they would tend to limit substitution between funds saved for different uses.

D. Formal Analysis of the Perfect Substitutes Assumption

How individuals in fact behave is an empirical question that cannot be answered by theory alone. Our approach in earlier formal analyses has been to test statistically whether IRAs and other forms of saving are treated as different, without trying to quantify the importance of, or even identify, the possible reasons. We have developed and estimated an econometric specification that encompasses both possibilities, that is, permitting flexible substitution. In particular, a special case of the specification is the perfect substitutes possibility. This constraint is strongly rejected by the data (Venti and Wise, 1986, 1987, 1990a, 1991b).

Even less extreme substitution implies that other saving should increase once the IRA limit has been reached. But this pattern is not observed in the data that we have analyzed, suggesting little substitution (Venti and Wise, 1991b).

As emphasized earlier, the simple theory leaves no role for the effect of advertising and other forms of promotion on IRA saving. Although it is difficult to quantify the effect of advertising, we are convinced that promotion played an important role in establishing the popularity of IRAs. To the extent that promotion is successful, it would tend to show up in our formal analysis as a preference for IRA saving over other forms of saving and as a rejection of the perfect substitutes assumption, as the data indicate.

To find that IRAs and other saving are not perfect substitutes is not anomalous but instead is consistent with other empirical findings on saving behavior. For example, one might expect that persons with firm pension plans would have lower balances in personal financial assets than persons without firm plans, controlling for personal attributes such as age and income. It might be presumed that firm pension benefits would substitute for personal saving. But the data do not show this. On the contrary, there is a tendency for those with firm pensions to have higher personal financial asset balances. The evidence is reviewed in Shefrin and Thaler (1988). What the data do seem to suggest, however, is that firm pensions reduce earnings by inducing earlier departure from the labor force. Instead of pension benefits substituting for personal saving, they may instead, by inducing earlier retirement, substitute for personal earnings, as emphasized in Lumsdaine and Wise (1990).

Closer to the IRA issue, it was presumed that IRAs would be more likely to be opened by persons without private pension plans, controlling for personal attributes such as income, age, and other financial asset balances. But the data do not show this tendency either; again, the IRA does not appear to be a substitute for firm pension plans (Venti and Wise, 1988).

We find that the simple model, which is the basis for much of the skepticism about the saving effect of IRAs, provides a poor description of actual IRA saving behavior. Simply economic theory provides an incomplete guide to saving behavior in other instances as well. Thus it should not be surprising if it were misleading in this instance. The primary tool of the simple theory is the rate of return. But the empirical evidence on balance shows little relationship between saving and observed rates of return (e.g., Bovenberg, 1989). Other factors apparently swamp whatever the effect of the return on new saving may be.[28] Per-

---

[28] It is even difficult to demonstrate a convincing relationship between rather wide-ranging individual tax rates and contributions to tax-deferred saving accounts, controlling for in-

sonal saving rates vary dramatically among countries but standard theory does not explain why. A plausible explanation is that habits, cultural norms, "taste" for saving, and the psychology of saving vary from country to country but are not incorporated in standard models.

Thus there is considerable motivation to look more broadly for explanations of saving behavior. Relaxation of the restrictive assumptions of the simple model is a start. But the data presented here suggest more, that a realistic explanation of saving must recognize much broader economic and psychological determinants of individual saving decisions.

DATA APPENDIX

Three sources of data were used to prepare tables and graphs in the text. Each data source and the principal adjustments that were made prior to calculation are described in this appendix.

1. Survey of Income and Program Participation (SIPP).   The SIPP is a large, ongoing survey of the U.S. population that is designed principally to collect data on the income and participation in government transfer programs. It is organized by annual panels, with each panel consisting of eight or nine interview waves administered at four-month intervals. Most of the SIPP data used here come from wave 7 of the 1984 panel (administered September to December 1985), wave 7 of the 1985 panel (January to April 1987), and wave 7 of the 1986 panel (January to April 1988). In the text tables and figures these three sources are referred to as 1985, 1986, and 1987 data respectively because they are closest to year-end balances in those years. It is clear, however, that for each panel the responses used may be as many as four months "off" from being year-end figures, as many as four months early in 1985 and four months late in 1986 and 1987. In all cases the IRA and other financial asset data pertain to assets owned by the reference person and the spouse; assets owned by other members of the household are excluded. *Financial assets excluding stocks and bonds* include regular (passbook) saving accounts, money market deposit accounts, certificates of deposit or other saving

---

come, age, and other tax filer characteristics. Feenberg and Skinner (1989) conclude that there is a positive relationship between marginal tax rates and IRA contributions, based on U.S. tax returns. Long (1990) also concludes that the relationship is positive. But Wise (1984) finds that the conclusion is extremely sensitive to the functional form used in the statistical analysis. Indeed, using precise marginal tax rates calculated from tax returns, he finds no relationship between individual marginal tax rates and contributions to Registered Retirement Saving Programs in Canada, controlling for income and other tax filer attributes, and using a specification that fits the data best. The evidence in Venti and Wise (1988) suggests that the marginal tax rate may be associated with whether a household contributes to an IRA but suggests little relationship to the amount of the contribution.

certificates, NOW or other interest bearing saving accounts, money market funds, U.S. government securities, municipal or corporate bonds, other interest earning assets, and noninterest bearing checking accounts. The category *financial assets including stocks and bonds* also includes the market value of stocks and mutual funds (less debt or margin account) and the face value of U.S. savings bonds. Note that the former category, despite its title, contains some bonds. This arises because we were unable to separate out bonds from other interest earning assets in the SIPP and we wanted to keep the names of asset groupings consistent with the categories derived from the other data sources.

2. Survey of Consumer Finances (SCF). The SCF is a panel survey first administered between February and July 1983. A subsample of the original sample was reinterviewed between June and September of 1986. The 1983 SCF is much smaller than the SIPP but contains more detail on financial assets. The 1986 reinterview contains less detail. In both 1983 and 1986 the special high-income sample is used. Details on the 1983 and 1986 SCF are available in Avery and Kennickell (1988a, 1988b). *Financial assets excluding stocks and bonds* include checking, statement savings, passbook, share, draft, and other saving accounts; money market accounts; and certificates of deposit. The category *financial assets including stocks and bonds* also includes stocks and all holdings of bonds including U.S. saving bonds.

3. Consumer Expenditure Surveys (CES). The CES is a quarterly panel survey used to obtain information on household expenditure patterns. Households enrolled in a quarter are followed for five quarters. We use CES data for all quarters from 1980:1 through 1989:1. For the calculations in this paper, we have combined all four quarterly reports into a single annual average. Thus, for example, the CES asset figure for 1983 will include balances reported for all 12 months in 1983. For this reason, and possibly others as well, annual figures obtained from the CES may differ from figures based on the other two sources, and from tax year data reported by the IRS. *Financial assets excluding stocks and bonds* includes saving accounts in banks, savings and loans, credit unions, and similar accounts; checking accounts, brokerage accounts, and other similar accounts; and U.S. savings bonds. The category *financial assets including stocks and bonds* also includes securities such as stocks, mutual funds, private bonds, government bonds, or treasury notes.

A key objective was to obtain from each data source a sample representative of the "IRA-eligible" U.S. population. The following steps are common to each source of data:

- Households in which the head or reference person is age sixty-five or older are deleted. The minimum age is determined by the availability of data for each source. In the CESs the minimum age of a household head is eighteen, in the SIPP the minimum age is twenty-one, and in the SCF the minimum age of a household head is twenty-five.
- Households in which the respondent or spouse of the respondent is self-employed are excluded. The self-employed had access to Keogh plans with contribution limits very different from the IRA limits. Elimination of the self-employed also minimizes a potential complication that arises because two of the surveys (the CESs and the 1986 SCF) ask respondents for combined IRA and Keogh balances.
- SIPP and SCF are weighted to represent the national population. The CES is weighted to represent the national urban population.

REFERENCES

Avery, Robert B., Gregory E. Elliehausen, and Thomas A. Gustafson (1986). "Pensions and Social Security in Household Portfolios: Evidence from the 1983 Survey of Consumer Finances." In Savings and Capital Formation. F. Gerald Adams and Susan M. Wachter, ed. Lexington, MA: Lexington Books.

Avery, Robert B., and Arthur B. Kennickell (1988a). *1986 Survey of Consumer Finances: Technical Manual and Codebook*. Board of Governors of the Federal Reserve System. November 9.

———(1988b). "Savings and Wealth: Evidence from the 1986 Survey of Consumer Finances." Paper presented at the Conference on Research in Income and Wealth. Washington, D.C. May 12–14.

Bosworth, Barry, Gary Burtless, and John Sabelhaus (1991). "The Decline in Saving: Evidence From Household Surveys." *Brookings Papers on Economic Activity*. 1:183–241. Washington, D.C.: Brookings Institution.

Bovenberg, A. Lans (1989). "Tax Policy and National Saving in the United States: A Survey." *National Tax Journal* 42,123–138.

Burman, Leonard, Joseph Cordes, and Larry Ozanne (1990). "IRAs and National Savings." *National Tax Journal*. 43,259–283.

Cagan, Philip (1965). *The Effect of Pension Plans on Aggregate Saving*. New York, National Bureau of Economic Research.

Employee Benefit Research Institute (1986). "Tax Reform and Employee Benefits." *Issue Brief* No. 59. October.

Feenberg, Daniel, and Jonathan Skinner (1989). "Sources of IRA Saving," *Tax Policy and the Economy* 3, 25–46.

Gale, William G., and John Karl Scholz (1990). "IRAs and Household Saving." Mimeo, University of Wisconsin.

Gravelle, Jane G. (1989). "Capital Gains Taxes, IRAs, and Savings." Congressional Research Service. September.

———. (1991). "Do Individual Retirement Accounts Increase Saving?" *Journal of Economic Perspectives* 5,133–149.

Hubbard, R. Glenn (1984). "Do IRAs and Keoghs Increase Saving?" *National Tax Journal*. 37, 43–54.

IRA Reporter (1988). *IRA Reporter* 6(9), September 30.

Joines, Douglas H., and James G. Manegold (1991). "IRAs and Saving: Evidence from a Panel of Taxpayers." University of Southern California, working paper No. 90-9.

Katona, George (1965). *Private Pensions and Individual Saving*. Ann Arbor: University of Michigan Press.

Kotlikoff, Laurence J. (1990). "The Crisis in U.S. Saving and Proposals to Address the Crisis." *National Tax Journal* 43,233–246.

Long, James E. (1990). "Marginal Tax Rates and IRA Contributions." *National Tax Journal* 43,143–153.

Lumsdaine, Robin L., and David A. Wise (1990). "Aging and Labor Force Participation: A Review of Trends and Explanations." National Bureau of Economic Research, working paper No. 3420 (August). Forthcoming in joint JCER-NBER conference volume. Chicago: University of Chicago Press.

Manchester, Joyce M., and James M. Poterba (1989). "Second Mortgages and Household Saving." *Regional Science and Urban Economics* 19,325–346.

Piacentini, Joseph S., and Timothy J. Cerino (1990). *EBRI Databook on Employee Benefits*. Washington, D.C.

Shefrin, Hersh M., and Richard H. Thaler (1988). "The Behavioral Life-Cycle Hypothesis." *Economic Inquiry* 26,609–643.

Skinner, Jonathan (1991). "Do IRAs Promote Saving? A Review of the Evidence." Mimeo, University of Virginia.

Summers, Lawrence H. (1986). "Issues in National Savings Policy." In *Savings and Capital Formation*. F. Gerald Adams and Susan M. Wachter, eds. Lexington, MA: Lexington Books.

Summers, Lawrence H., and Chris Carroll (1987). "Why is U.S. National Saving So Low?" *Brookings Papers on Economic Activity* 2,607–635.

Thaler, Richard H. (1990). "Saving, Fungibility, and Mental Accounts." *Journal of Economic Perspectives* 4,193–205.

Venti, Steven F., and David A. Wise 91986). "Tax-Deferred Accounts, Constrained Choice and Estimation of Individual Saving." *Review of Economic Studies* 53, 579–601.

_____(1987). "IRAs and Saving." In *The Effects of Taxation on Capital Accumulation*. Martin Feldstein, ed. Chicago: University of Chicago Press.

_____ (1988). "The Determinants of IRA Contributions and the Effect of Limit Changes." In *Pensions in the U.S. Economy*. Z. Bodie, J. Shoven, and D. Wise, eds. Chicago University of Chicago Press.

_____ (1990a). "Have IRAs Increased U.S. Saving?: Evidence from the Consumer Expenditure Surveys." *Quarterly Journal of Economics* 105,661–698.

_____(1990b). "Heterogeneity, Individual Effects, and IRA Saving: Further Evidence From SIPP." Mimeo.

_____(1991a). "Aging and the Income Value of Housing Wealth." *Journal of Public Economics*. 44:371–395.

_____(1991b). "The Saving Effect of Tax-Deferred Retirement Accounts: Evidence From SIPP." In *National Saving and Economic Performance*. B. Douglas Bernheim and John Shoven, eds. Chicago: University of Chicago Press.

Wachter, Susan M., ed. *Savings and Capital Formation*. Lexington MA: Lexington Books.

Wise, David A. (1984). "The Effects of Policy Change on RRSP Contributions." Mimeo, prepared for the Tax Policy and Legislation Branch of the Canadian Department of Finance.

WHY DIDN'T THE TAX REFORM ACT OF 1986 RAISE CORPORATE TAXES?

James M. Poterba
MIT and NBER

EXECUTIVE SUMMARY

The Tax Reform Act of 1986 was projected to raise corporate taxes by more than $120 billion over the 1986 to 1991 period. Actual federal corporate tax receipts in the last five years have fallen far short of these projections. This paper explores the factors that have contributed to this shortfall. The most important factor is lower-than-expected corporate profits. The underperformance of corporate profits can be attributed to three principal causes. First, the predicted rates of corporate profits when the 1986 Tax Reform Act was enacted were high by historical standards. The total returns on corporate capital in the U.S. economy in the late 1980s were not as high as the pre-1986 forecasts which underlay initial revenue projections. Second, corporate interest payments were significantly higher, as a share of corporate operating income or GNP, in the late 1980s than in the years leading up to the Tax Reform Act. This reduced the corporate tax base, and may in substantial part ultimately be attributable to the marginal incentive effects for debt and equity finance provided in the 1986 Tax Reform Act. Third, also quite likely in reaction to recent tax changes, the last few years

I am grateful to the National Science Foundation for research support, to David Frankel for excellent research assistance, and to Ken Petrick of the Bureau of Economic Analysis and Sandra Byberg of the Internal Revenue Service for data assistance. This paper was prepared for the NBER Conference on Tax Policy and the Economy, November 19, 1991.

have seen rapid growth in the income reported by Subchapter S corporations. This income is taxed under the individual income tax. The rise of S corporations has, therefore, contributed to the erosion of the corporate income tax.

The Tax Reform Act of 1986 was forecast to raise corporate taxes by nearly $120 billion between 1986 and 1991. Actual corporate tax receipts have fallen below projections in each of these years. In February 1987, the Congressional Budget Office (CBO) forecast federal corporate tax collections of $138 billion for fiscal year 1990. Actual receipts were $94 billion. The corporate tax shortfall has exacerbated the federal deficit and raised fundamental questions about the long-term revenue potential of the corporate income tax.

This paper examines the reasons for the corporate tax shortfall. The paper is divided into five sections. The first summarizes the predicted effects of the Tax Reform Act of 1986 and the actual pattern of corporate tax collections in the last five years. It shows that TRA86 did raise federal corporate tax collections relative to what they would have been otherwise, but that a decline in corporate profits relative to their predicted level depressed corporate tax receipts.

Section II examines the source of the decline in corporate profits in more detail, identifying a component due to a reduction in the total return to capital, and a component due to an increase in the fraction of corporate earnings paid out as interest. Higher interest charges are the most important factor in the late-1980s decline in corporate profits. If corporate leverage had been constant at its 1986 level relative to earnings, then cumulative corporate tax receipts over the 1987 to 1991 period would have been $42 billion (1991) dollars above their actual level.

Section III analyzes another post-1986 trend that has contributed to the corporate tax shortfall: The shift from C to S corporations. This shift accounts for a significant decline in corporate taxes, particularly in 1990 and 1991. This shift may in large part be the result of changes in the relative tax rates on individuals and corporations in the 1986 Tax Reform Act, notably the introduction of a top tax rate on individuals below that on corporations.

The fourth section analyzes how the Tax Reform Act of 1986 affected the effective tax rate on corporate capital, and what accounts for disparities between the statutory and effective rate. This section employs a methodology developed in Auerbach and Poterba (1987) to analyze the 1986 changes in the structure of corporate taxation. The conclusion speculates about the future revenue prospects of the corporate income tax.

I. CORPORATE TAX RECEIPTS, 1959–1990

The 1986 Tax Reform Act (TRA) raised corporate taxes in the year when it was enacted, and it was projected to increase corporate taxes for the remainder of the 1980s.[1] TRA reduced the statutory tax rate on corporate taxable income, but more than compensated for the associated revenue loss by eliminating the investment tax credit, lengthening depreciation lifetimes for many assets, and adopting a variety of other base-broadeners. Table 1 shows the forecasts made by the Congressional Budget Office in their *Economic and Budget Outlook* each February, as well as the actual pattern of corporate tax recepits. Actual revenues have fallen below projections, even one year ahead, in every year since 1986. The revenue shortfall began in 1987, widened in 1988, and then rose sharply in 1990 when actual revenues fell below 1989 collections. The table shows that the revenue shortfall is more than a failure of the TRA to increase revenues as predicted. In each fiscal year since 1987, actual tax receipts fell below the CBO's projections from before the Tax Reform Act of 1986 was enacted.[2]

There are two differences between the forecasts in early 1986 and those in early 1987, the passage of the Tax Reform Act, and changes in forecasts of corporate profits. Corporate profits are defined in this discussion as economic profits, which equals reported profits with corrections for the inventory valuation adjustment and the capital consumption adjustment.[3] Table 2 shows the projected share of corporate profits in GNP in early 1986, and early 1987, as well as the actual values for calendar years 1987 to 1991. The CBO's forecast prior to the passage of TRA86 assumed that corporate profits would average more than 8 percent of GNP for the 1987 to 1991 period. One year later, projected corporate profits were much lower, averaging 7.2 percent of GNP. This downward revision reduced the projected level of corporate taxes. The last column of Table 2 shows that actual corporate profits averaged just over 6 per-

---

[1] One important component of the Tax Reform Act was a lengthening of depreciation life times. Longer asset lives raise taxes in the near term but reduce them in future years, when assets that would otherwise have been fully depreciated are still generating deductions.

[2] The corporate tax shortfall has attracted attention from tax policy makers. The U.S. Senate Committee on Finance (1990) held hearings to assess the reasons for the shortfall. Testimony presented at the hearings discusses the explanations for the profit decline that are developed in this paper as well as other possibilities.

[3] The IVA removes spurious profits due to changes in the value of inventories and work-in-progress from the profit concept, while the CCA corrects accounting depreciation to reflect economic depreciation measured at replacement cost.

TABLE 1.
Forecast and Actual Federal Corporate Tax Receipts, FY 1986–1991.

Fiscal year	Actual receipts	Pre-TRA projection	1/87	Projected receipts as of:			
				2/88	1/89	1/90	1/91
1987	84	89	101				
1988	94	100	119	99			
1989	103	108	126	107	103		
1990	94	112	138	119	112	102	
1991	98*	114	151	126	120	111	99
1987	1.9	2.0	2.3				
1988	2.0	2.1	2.5	2.1			
1989	2.0	2.1	2.5	2.1	2.0		
1990	1.7	2.0	2.5	2.2	2.1	1.9	
1991	1.8	1.9	2.6	2.2	2.1	1.9	1.8

Source: Column 1 is drawn from the Congressional Budget Office, *The Economic and Budget Outlook: January 1991,* Table D-4. Column 2 is from the February 1986 CBO publication *The Economic and Budget Outlook.* Other columns are from intervening CBO publications dated as shown.

cent of GNP between 1987 and 1991, declining from 6.8 percent in 1987 to just over 5 percent in the first half of 1991.

The decline in corporate profits explains a large fraction of the corporate tax shortfall. Applying a marginal tax rate of 34 percent to profits to compute federal corporate tax receipts would suggest that a 1.7 percent of GNP decline in corporate profits, the difference between the January 1987 CBO forecast and actual profits for calendar 1991, would reduce corporate taxes by approximately 0.6 percent of GNP. The actual difference between the CBO's 1987 forecast and actual 1990 receipts was 0.8

TABLE 2.
Forecast and Actual Corporate Profits/GNP, CY 1987–1991.

Year	Forecast 2/86	Forecast 1/87	Actual
1987	8.1	7.2%	6.8
1988	8.2	7.1	6.9
1989	8.2	7.1	6.0
1990	8.1	7.2	5.5
1991	7.9	7.2	5.1*

Source: Column 1 is drawn from the Congressional Budget Office, *Economic and Budget Outlook: Fiscal Years 1987–1991* (February 1986), the second column from the similar publication dated January 1991, and the final column from the National Income and Product Accounts. The starred entry for 1991 is based on only two quarters of data.

percent of GNP. This preliminary calculation thus suggests that changes in corporate profitability have been a key factor in the reduction in corporate taxes.

II. WHY HAVE CORPORATE PROFITS FALLEN?

Profits vary as a result of fluctuations in operating earnings or because of changes in the share of earnings paid out as interest. The two sources of profit shocks imply different interpretations of a reduction in corporate taxes as a result of a profit decline. If the total returns from capital decline, then a decline in corporate profits coincide with a decline in the total revenue that can be collected from the corporate sector. If, however, the profit decline is the result of higher interest payments, then the decline in corporate taxes will be offset in part by higher tax collections on interest recipients.

Table 3 presents summary data on the role of interest payments and declining operating profits in explaining the decline in corporate profits. The first column displays corporate profits as a percentage of GNP, while the second shows corporate capital income, the sum of profits and interest payments, to GNP. Corporate capital income as a share of GNP has remained relatively stable, averaging 8.4 percent over the last five years, while corporate profits have declined from 6.7 percent in 1986 to 5.5 percent in 1991. This reflects the increase in the share of corporate capital income distributed as interest: 18.6 percent in 1986 and 32.4 percent in 1991. Corporate interest payments as a share of GNP rose from 1.5 percent (1986) to 2.6 percent (1990) during this period.

The rise in interest payout is due primarily to changes in corporate leverage. Nominal interest rates were somewhat higher in 1990 than in 1986, but not by enough to explain the rise in the interest payout ratio in Table 3.[4] Between 1986 and 1990, however, U.S. nonfinancial corporations repurchased $476 billion of corporate equity, and issued $758 billion of debt. Share repurchases peaked in 1988, when these firms bought back shares worth $130 billion. This pattern of equity repurchase by nonfinancial firms has attracted widespread attention, but it is only partly responsible for the increase in interest payouts from U.S. corporations. Approximately two-thirds of the increase in net interest payments is concentrated among financial firms.

---

[4] The nominal interest rate on ten-year Treasury bonds averaged 7.68% in 1986, compared with 8.55% in 1990. The differential is a measure of the shift in the structure of interest rates affecting corporate borrowers.

TABLE 3.
Corporate Operating Income and Profits, 1960–1990.

Year	(Profits + Interest)/GNP	Interest/GNP	Profits/GNP
1960	9.6	0.0	9.6
1961	9.4	0.0	9.4
1962	10.2	0.0	10.1
1963	10.6	0.1	10.5
1964	10.9	0.1	10.9
1965	11.7	0.2	11.5
1966	11.6	0.4	11.2
1967	10.8	0.5	10.3
1968	10.7	0.5	10.2
1969	9.9	0.8	9.1
1970	8.4	1.1	7.4
1971	8.9	1.0	7.9
1972	9.2	0.9	8.3
1973	9.2	0.9	8.3
1974	8.2	1.3	6.9
1975	8.6	1.3	7.4
1976	9.0	0.9	8.1
1977	9.8	1.0	8.8
1978	9.9	1.1	8.8
1979	9.4	1.4	8.0
1980	8.4	1.9	6.5
1981	8.2	2.1	6.2
1982	6.9	2.2	4.7
1983	8.2	1.9	6.3
1984	8.9	1.8	7.1
1985	8.7	1.7	7.0
1986	8.2	1.5	6.7
1987	8.5	1.7	6.8
1988	8.6	1.7	6.9
1989	8.4	2.4	6.0
1990	8.0	2.6	5.5
1960–69	10.5	0.3	10.2
1970–79	8.2	1.0	7.2
1980–85	8.2	1.9	6.3
1986–90	8.3	2.0	6.3

Source: National Income and Product Accounts.

Until the mid-1980s, U.S. firms typically issued a small amount of equity each year. The shift in financial policy is at least in part attributable to the 1981 and 1986 tax reforms. Table 4 shows the net-of-tax returns individual investors in debt and equity could earn in various years since 1980. The table follows the tradition of Merton Miller's (1977) focus on the after-tax returns to investors at the top of the income distri-

TABLE 4.
Tax Incentives for Corporate Leverage, 1975–1990.

Year	After-Tax Return on Debt	After-Tax Return on Equity	Equity − Debt Differential
1975	.30	.315	.015
1980	.30	.332	.032
1985	.50	.392	−.108
1990	.72	.545	−.175

Source: Author's calculations. The first column reports $(1 - m^*)$, where m^* denotes the marginal federal income tax rate on interest income received by the highest income individual investors. The second column reports $(1 - \tau_{corp})^*(1 - .5m^* - .5\tau_{cg})$ where τ_{corp} denotes the statutory corporate tax rate and τ_{cg} the effective capital gains tax rate, defined as .25 times the statutory capital gains tax rate facing realized gains for top-bracket households. The .25 factor reflects the reduction in the effective tax rate as a result of deferral and basis step-up at death.

bution. The after-tax return on debt is $(1 - \tau_{max})$, where τ_{max} is the personal income tax rate on an individual facing the top marginal tax rate. The after-tax equity return is $(1 - \tau_{corp})^*(\lambda(1 - \tau_{div}) + (1 - \lambda)(1 - \tau_{cg}))$, reflecting both the corporate tax burden and the effect of shareholder taxes on dividends and capital gains.

Table 4 shows the sharp increase in the relative return on debt as opposed to equity finance. In 1980, the after-tax equity return for top bracket investors was significantly higher than that from investments in debt. This pattern was reversed by the end of the decade, when sharp reductions in the individual top marginal rate made the debt return more attractive than the equity return.[5]

When corporate profits decline because of higher interest payout, the net effect on federal revenue depends on the marginal tax rate of the interest recipient. It is difficult to measure the net revenue cost of higher interest payout, because this requires information on the tax brackets of these recipients. On average, as Gordon and Slemrod (1988) argue, interest is received by taxpayers with lower marginal tax rates than the interest payers. If the recipients are tax-exempt institutions, then the revenue cost is the full amount of the foregone corporate income taxes. If, however, the recipients are households, with an average marginal tax rate on interest income of more than 20 percent, then the net revenue cost of higher corporate interest payments are much smaller.

---

[5] The tax incentives for debt versus equity finance are sensitive to assumptions about the investor's identity. For tax-exempt institutions, for example, the return to debt has been constant throughout the 1980s, while the return to equity has increased as a result of reductions in the corporate tax rate.

III. THE RISE OF SUBCHAPTER S STATUS

Another factor that has affected the level of corporate profits, particularly in the last two years, is the channelling of some income that would have been corporate before 1986 into noncorporate form. Many enterprises have some flexibility in choosing whether to incorporate, and to pay taxes as a C corporation, or to face the individual income tax code as an S corporation. C corporate income is taxed once at the corporate rate and again when it is distributed to shareholders.

Just as the 1981 and 1986 tax reforms altered the relative tax burdens on debt and equity finance, they altered the incentives for choosing C versus S corporation status. Gordon and Mackie-Mason (1991) and Nelson (1991) provide detailed summaries of the somewhat conflicting incentives in the recent tax reform. The principal effects are as follows. First, when the marginal personal tax rate falls relative to the corporate rate, it becomes more attractive to use Subchapter S status. Because the 1986 tax reform significantly reduced individual tax rates, it should provide a strong incentive for increased use of S corporations. Second, the 1986 reform repealed the General Utilities doctrine, making it more costly to hold appreciating assets in corporate form. There are some offsetting effects that make S status less attractive than C status for some activities, but the primary effect was to increase the incentive for organizing S status corporations.

Gordon and Mackie-Mason (1991) present preliminary evidence on the effects of the 1986 tax reform on C versus S corporate status. They document a sharp increase in S incorporations immediately after the tax reform, and show that this organizational form has continued to grow more rapidly in subsequent years. They also observe the difficulty of using net income reported by S and C corporations as measures of their relative size, because there are strong incentives for choosing one or the other organizational form based on whether a particular project is expected to generate income or losses.

Table 5 reports increase in the amount of income reported by S corporations during the 1980s. In 1980, S corporations reported only 2 percent as much income as C corporations. By 1986 this percentage had increased to 5 percent. Actual data are not available for years after 1988, but IRS projections suggest a continuing sharp increase to 18 percent in 1990. If the net income projected to be reported by S corporations had been reported by C corporations in 1990, ordinary corporate income tax receipts would have been higher by approximately 13 percent. The issue this table cannot resolve is whether the income that has been reported by S corporations would otherwise have been reported by C corporations.

TABLE 5.
The Rise of S Corporations.

| Year | Net Income/NFC Net Assets | | | Increase in NFC Taxes if all S Corps were Cs |
	C Corporations	S Corporations	Ratio	
1980	4.9%	0.1%	0.02	0.04%
1981	4.3	0.1	0.01	0.03
1982	2.8	0.1	0.04	0.03
1983	3.9	0.2	0.04	0.05
1984	5.5	0.2	0.04	0.06
1985	5.7	0.2	0.04	0.06
1986	5.3	0.3	0.05	0.07
1987	5.5	0.7	0.13	0.26
1988	7.1	0.9	0.13	0.28
1989	6.8	1.0	0.15	0.33
1990	6.5	1.2	0.18	0.37

Source: Columns 1 and 2 are from author's tabulations from various issues of the *SOI Bulletin*. Column 3 is the ratio of columns 1 and 2. Column 4 is the product of column 2 and the average tax rate on C corporate income. Data for 1989 and 1990 are based on IRS projections.

The timing of the rise in S corporate income, and its coincidence with the change in the tax law, suggests that there has been a shift from C to S corporate status and that this has reduced reported corporate profits.

Switching productive activities out of the corporate sector reduces corporate profits, but it also raises the income reported under the personal income tax. Nelson (1991) presents some evidence on the difference between the statutory corporate tax rate and the tax rate at which S corporate income is reported. The net effect of C to S corporate switching on total federal revenue may be substantially smaller than the estimated effects on corporate taxes alone.

IV. EFFECTIVE TAX RATES VS. STATUTORY TAX RATES: THE POST-1986 EXPERIENCE

A central issue in evaluating how an increase in interest payout or a decrease in profits within the corporate sector will affect revenue is the choice of the tax rate to apply to foregone profits. One obvious choice is the maximum statutory marginal rate, currently 34 percent. The difficulty with this choice is that some firms face lower marginal rates, and some, with loss carryforwards, may face a current marginal tax rate of zero on incremental earnings. An alternative choice is the effective tax rate, the average rate that applies to taxable income reported to the IRS.

This section explores the evolution of the effective tax rate relative to the statutory tax rate since 1986.

Auerbach and Poterba (1987) computed effective tax rates, compared them with statutory tax rates, and developed a framework for decomposing the difference between the two. That analysis focused on nonfinancial corporations (NFCs), because these firms were most directly affected by the tax reforms of 1981 and 1986. To compare the experience of NFCs with that of the entire corporate sector, Table 6 shows the net corporate tax payments by NFCs.[6] The first column reports the NFC's real corporate tax payments, while the second and third columns scale these tax payments by GNP and corporate assets. Tax receipts from NFCs in the last five years were only slightly higher relative to GNP than in the first five years of the 1980s, when this share averaged 1.4 percent. The last column focuses on tax payments divided by net assets. This ratio, which averaged 4.6 percent during the first five years of the 1960s, was only 2 percent in the late 1980s. Corporate taxes have increased relative to corporate assets since 1986. For the first five years of the 1980s, NFC tax payments were only 1.5 percent of tangible assets. During the second half of the decade, they averaged 2.0 percent. In 1986, the Tax Reform Act was projected to increase tax collections from 2.5 percent to 3.0 percent of corporate assets in 1990.

The detailed decomposition of differences between the statutory and average effective tax rate is presented in Table 7. The first column shows the maximum statutory tax rate for each year from 1959 to 1988, the last year with complete IRS data for performing the analysis. The entries in the six middle columns describe how various factors have caused the average tax rate to differ from the statutory rate. Negative entries indicate factors that caused the average tax rate to be less than the statutory rate, and positive entries correspond to factors that increased the tax burden above the statutory rate. The average tax rate, taxes/profits, is reported in the last column. It is the sum of the maximum statutory tax rate plus the six adjustment factors in the middle columns.

The first source of differences between statutory and average tax rates, capital recovery provisions that are more or less generous than economic depreciation, is shown in the second column of Table 7. This column includes the tax reduction from use of the investment tax credit, as well as that due to differences between tax depreciation and true economic depreciation. During the early 1980s, capital recovery provisions ac-

---

[6] The table measures tax payments net of refunds obtained by loss carrybacks, including taxes collected as a result of audits or other retabulations. The appendix to Auerbach and Poterba (1987) provides a more detailed description.

TABLE 6.
Federal Corporate Tax Receipts from NFCs, 1960–1990.

Year	Federal receipts from NFCs ($1990)	NFC taxes as a percentage of:	
		GNP	NFC assets
1960	76.5	3.49	4.33
1961	76.8	3.41	4.31
1962	77.8	3.29	4.37
1963	86.1	3.49	4.81
1964	88.5	3.41	4.86
1965	98.2	3.58	5.28
1966	102.6	3.54	5.30
1967	92.6	3.10	4.53
1968	105.9	3.40	5.06
1969	98.4	3.09	4.53
1970	74.2	2.33	3.31
1971	77.4	2.37	3.40
1972	81.7	2.38	3.50
1973	91.7	2.54	3.79
1974	86.9	2.42	3.19
1975	76.2	2.15	2.56
1976	91.5	2.46	3.01
1977	96.3	2.48	3.10
1978	100.6	2.45	3.04
1979	93.7	2.23	2.62
1980	80.3	1.92	2.09
1981	65.8	1.54	1.63
1982	38.6	0.93	0.95
1983	54.2	1.26	1.34
1984	65.9	1.43	1.63
1985	59.5	1.25	1.49
1986	61.8	1.26	1.58
1987	79.5	1.57	2.05
1988	83.5	1.58	2.15
1989	83.2	1.54	2.18
1990	77.7	1.42	2.04
1960–69	90.3	3.3	4.4
1970–79	87.0	2.3	3.1
1980–85	60.7	1.4	1.3
1986–90	77.1	1.5	2.0

Source: Author's tabulations as described in the text.

counted for a 22 percent differential between the statutory and the average tax rate. This disparity was reduced substantially by the 1986 Tax Reform Act, which eliminated the investment tax credit and reduced the generosity of other capital recovery provisions. By 1988, the last year for which IRS data are available, capital recovery reduced the average tax

TABLE 7.
Statutory vs. Average Effective Tax Rates, 1970–1988.

Year	τ	λ	Capital Consumption, Adjustment, Investment, & Credits	IVA & DebtGain	NOL & NTI & Carrybacks	FTC and Foreign Income	Progressivity	Retabulations	Average Tax Rate
					Components of Difference between Statutory & Average Rate				
1970	49.2	0.935	-9.58	-2.09	7.73	0.66	-3.20	2.22	44.93
1971	48	0.939	-8.26	-4.98	6.25	0.35	-2.93	2.12	40.56
1972	48	0.940	-10.39	-1.76	3.97	1.09	-2.88	1.97	40.00
1973	48	0.945	-11.28	0.53	3.17	3.47	-2.64	1.90	43.15
1974	48	0.956	-13.11	8.03	4.76	-0.21	-2.11	1.91	47.27
1975	48	0.940	-7.38	-4.68	4.36	-0.06	-2.89	1.57	38.91
1976	48	0.946	-7.83	0.53	3.46	-0.19	-2.60	1.62	43.00
1977	48	0.944	-9.53	-0.90	3.23	-0.86	-2.69	1.01	38.25
1978	48	0.936	-11.39	-0.18	3.05	0.75	-3.09	1.64	38.77
1979	46	0.933	-10.38	3.77	3.94	-4.64	-3.09	1.38	36.99
1980	46	0.928	-13.28	4.21	6.90	0.18	-3.33	1.91	42.58
1981	46	0.926	-18.73	0.02	10.51	1.46	-3.40	1.87	37.73
1982	46	0.917	-27.20	-2.43	18.21	0.31	-3.83	2.53	33.59
1983	46	0.920	-24.89	-0.65	12.08	0.08	-3.69	5.13	34.06
1984	46	0.916	-22.09	-1.53	9.28	0.27	-3.88	1.64	29.68
1985	46	0.912	-25.44	-2.60	11.11	-1.15	-4.06	2.06	25.93
1986	46	0.890	-19.27	-5.12	11.21	0.27	-5.05	1.69	29.73
1987	40	0.948	-13.59	-0.65	9.59	1.41	-2.09	2.92	37.58
1988	34	1.003	-7.75	-1.05	3.88	-0.20	0.09	1.34	30.31

Notes: τ denotes the statutory tax rate, λ the tax progressivity parameter (λ = Taxes Paid/(Taxable Income)/τ), and the various contributory factors to differences between statutory and effective tax rates are described in the text. IVA is the inventory valuation adjustment, NOL stands for Net Operating Losses, NTI denotes nontaxable income, and FTC denotes the Foreign Tax Credit.

rate by only 7.7 percent. This marks a return to roughly the conditions of the 1960s, when capital recovery reduced the average tax rate by 8.9 percent.

The third column in Table 7 reports the effect of inflation on average tax rates. This column combines two separate influences. First, inflation leads to spurious inventory profits that raise corporate tax payments and the average tax rate.[7] Inflation also exerts a countervailing effect on the average tax rate by reducing the real value of corporate debt, thus generating capital gains for equity holders. These gains are untaxed, so inflation raises economic income but does not affect taxes. The two effects roughly cancel, resulting in a small net effect of inflation on the average tax rate. Inflation raised the average tax rate by less than 1 percent during the 1970s. It reduced the average tax rate by 2.3 percent during the 1986 to 1988 period.

The fourth column in Table 7 indicates the impact of imperfect loss offset provisions on the average tax rate. The principal effect of imperfect loss offset is to raise the average tax rate when firms experience losses, because firms with negative income cannot claim tax refunds. Tax receipts are therefore higher than they would be in a system with proportional taxation of economic income. This effect is somewhat attenuated by the availability of loss carrybacks and net operating loss carryforwards. Carrybacks allow some loss offset in the year when losses occur. Loss carryforwards, in contrast, reduce a firm's current tax liability as a result of previous losses.

Imperfect loss-offset provisions may raise or lower the average tax rate, depending on whether net operating loss deductions exceed the value of losses not carried back. The entries in column 7 of Table 4 show that the impact of loss provisions has declined in the post-1985 period. By 1988, these considerations raised the average corporate tax rate by less than 4 percent, while they had averaged a 12.7 percent increase during the 1982 to 1985 period. Losses had a much greater affect in the early 1980s than in any other period.

The decline in the incidence of losses since 1986 has contributed to a reduction in the average corporate tax rate, holding other things constant. While the factors that reduced the prevalence of losses, for example the less generous tax depreciation provisions in this period, have raised corporate taxes, the reduction in losses as a result of these provisions actually blunts their net effect on revenues.

The fifth column of Table 7 describes how foreign tax provisions affect

---

[7] Inflation's positive impact through a related channel, the failure to index depreciation allowances for inflation, is subsumed in the capital recovery term.

the average tax rate. This term consists of two parts. The first measures the increase in taxes that would have resulted if foreign source income were taxable at the U.S. statutory rate, and the second reduces taxes by the amount of foreign tax credits claimed. If the statutory tax rates in all other countries equaled that in the United States and all firms could utilize foreign tax credits in full, then the net foreign tax effect in our table would equal zero. If foreign countries levied taxes at rates below the domestic rate, the foreign tax effect would be positive because the domestic taxes on foreign source income would exceed the foreign tax credit. The net effect of foreign tax provisions is a small increase in the average tax rate, with relatively little change between the early 1980s and the most recent years.

The sixth and seventh columns of Table 7 indicate the influence of two other factors, tax progressivity and retabulations, on the average tax rate. Tax progressivity, which accounts for the fact that some corporate income is taxed at rates below the statutory maximum, lowered the average tax rate by roughly 4 percent in the years preceding the 1986 Tax Reform Act. The progressivity effect became much smaller in 1988, with effectively *no* reduction in the average tax rate. This pattern deserves further exploration, but it could be a result of the previously noted shift from C to S corporations. This shift may have occurred disproportionately among small enterprises that previously may have faced marginal tax rates below the statutory corporate rate.

The final category, for retabulations, typically raises the average corporate tax rate. This reflects the impact of audits. There is no substantial change in the importance of this effect in the period since 1986.

Table 7 clearly suggests that the most important factor that historically led average tax rates to fall below the statutory rate is capital recovery. In the early 1980s, capital recovery provisions depressed the average tax rate by 14% more than they did during the 1960s and by 13 percent more than during the late 1970s. In large part because the 1986 Tax Reform Act reduced the generosity of tax depreciation, capital recovery factors today have a much smaller effect in reducing the effective average tax rate.

The most obvious conclusion from Table 7 is that the average effective tax rate has been closer to the statutory maximum rate in the post-1986 period than in any earlier time. In 1988, the average effective rate was less than 4 percent lower than the statutory rate, compared with a difference of more than 20% in 1985. These statistics confirm our earlier conclusion that the shortfall in corporate taxes since 1986 is not the result of differences between the projected and actual effective rate, but rather due to factors that have reduced the amount of corporate profits available for corporate taxation.

V. CONCLUSIONS

Corporate tax receipts during the last five years have fallen significantly below projections that were made when the Tax Reform Act of 1986 was enacted. These projections called for a substantial increase in corporate taxes during the last half of the 1980s. Actual corporate tax receipts have barely equalled the level projected in early 1986, before passage of the tax reforms that were expected to increase revenues.

The most important factor in the corporate tax shortfall is lower-than-expected corporate profits. The underperformance of corporate profits can be attributed to three principal factors. First, the predicted rates of corporate profits when the 1986 Tax Reform Act was enacted were high by historical standards. The total returns on corporate capital in the U.S. economy in the late 1980s were not as high as the pre-1986 forecasts which underlay initial revenue projections. Second, as a share of corporate operating income or GNP, corporate interest payments were significantly higher in the late 1980s than in the years leading up to the Tax Reform Act. This reduced the corporate tax base, and may, in substantial part, ultimately be attributable to the marginal incentive effects for debt and equity finance provided in the 1986 Tax Reform Act. Third, also quite likely in reaction to recent tax changes, the last few years have seen rapid growth in the income reported by Subchapter S corporations. This income is taxed under the individual income tax. The rise of S corporations, therefore, has contributed to the erosion of the corporate income tax.

The most important unsettled issue this paper raises is how to calculate the net revenue effect of the various behavioral shifts described herein. A decline in corporate profits that results from higher interest payouts reduces corporate income tax revenues, but at the same time may increase the tax collections from interest recipients. A similar shift in the labeling of revenue occurs when enterprises choose to become Subchapter S corporations. It is essential to net the decline in corporate taxes against the increase in other taxes in evaluating the revenue effects. This requires a set of assumptions about the marginal recipients of interest payments, and about the types of activity that are shifted between C and S corporate status. Further research is needed to provide such models.

The experience of the last several years underscores the elasticity of taxable income flows among different labels with different tax characteristics. When the tax code places different burdens on debt and equity or S and C corporate income, some taxpayers are likely to respond by rechanneling their taxable income. The elasticity of such financial flows is far greater than the behavioral elasticities, say of labor supply or saving, because the real effects associated with financial relabeling are less substantial than those with changing a factor such as labor supply.

REFERENCES

Auerbach, Alan J., and James M. Poterba (1987). "Why have Corporate Tax Revenues Declined?," In *Tax Policy and the Economy*, vol. 1, 3–29. Lawrence H. Summers, ed. Cambridge: The MIT Press.

Board of Governors of the Federal Reserve System (1991). *Balance Sheets of the U.S. Economy*. Washington, D.C.: Board of Governors.

Gordon, Roger G., and Joel B. Slemord (1988). "Is Revenue Collected from Taxing Capital Income?" In *Tax Policy and the Economy*, vol. 2, 89–130. Lawrence H. Summers, ed. Cambridge: The MIT Press.

Gordon, Roger G., and Jeffrey Mackie-Mason (1991). "Effects of the Tax Reform Act of 1986 on Corporate Financial Policy and Organizational Form." In *Do Taxes Matter? The Impact of the Tax Reform Act of 1986*, 91–131. Joel B. Slemrod, ed. Cambridge: The MIT Press.

Miller, Merton H. (1977). "Debt and Taxes," *Journal of Finance* 32, 261–275.

Nelson, Susan C. (1991). "S Corporations Since the Tax Reform Act of 1986." U.S. Department of the Treasury, Office of Tax Analysis, Washington D.C.

U.S. Congressional Budget Office (1986). *The Economic and Budget Outlook: An Update*. Washington, D.C.: U.S. Government Printing Office.

U.S. Congressional Budget Office, (1991). *The Economic and Budget Outlook*. Washington, D.C.: U.S. Government Printing Office.

U.S. Senate, Committee on Finance (1990). *Decline of Corporate Tax Revenues: Hearing Before the Committee on Finance*, May 3. Washington, D.C.: U.S. Government Printing Office.

CARBON TAX DESIGN AND U.S. INDUSTRY PERFORMANCE

Lawrence H. Goulder
Stanford University and NBER

EXECUTIVE SUMMARY

This paper examines the effects of a U.S. carbon tax on U.S. industries. We consider alternative tax designs that differ according to the tax treatment of internationally traded goods and the use of tax revenues. The effects of these policy options are explored with a dynamic general equilibrium model of the United States that incorporates international trade.

In general, the burden of a U.S. carbon tax is fairly highly concentrated among a few industries. For these industries, the magnitude of the burden depends critically on the way the tax is designed. The costs to these industries in terms of profits and output are much lower when the tax is introduced on a destination basis (i.e., based on carbon emissions associated with the consumption or use of fuels) than when it is introduced on an origin basis (i.e., based on emissions associated with the production or supply of fuels). On the other hand, for a given tax rate the economy-wide costs are higher when the tax is destination-

This paper was prepared for the NBER Conference on Tax Policy and the Economy, Washington, D.C., November 19, 1991. I am grateful to Lans Bovenberg, Harry Huizinga, Alan Manne, Ron McKinnon, Jim Poterba, and Robert Staiger for helpful suggestions, to Miguel Cruz for excellent research assistance, and to the National Science Foundation (Grant SES-9011722) and Stanford University Center for Economic Policy Research for financial support.

based, reflecting the fact that the nation's "emissions consumption" exceeds its "emissions production."

There are various degrees to which policy makers could implement the destination principle in a carbon tax. This choice critically influences the extent to which the tax preserves "international competitiveness" as well as the administrative feasibility of the tax. One option is to apply the destination principle selectively, imposing the tax on the limited number of carbon-based products with "significant" carbon content. This gives rise to a partial destination-based tax. Such a tax would avert the most serious potential costs in terms of international competitiveness while avoiding the substantial administrative costs that a full destination-based carbon tax could entail. At the same time, the partial destination-based tax could achieve over 90 percent of the reduction in U.S.-consumption-related emissions that would occur under the full destination-based tax.

Using carbon tax revenues to finance cuts in pre-existing distortionary taxes reduces, but does not eliminate, the adverse consequences of the carbon tax policy for industry profits and investment. Aggregate efficiency results suggest that a carbon tax must inevitably generate losses to at least some industries.

I. INTRODUCTION

The past few years have witnessed a dramatic increase in concerns about the extent to which emissions of carbon dioxide (CO_2) and other greenhouse gases might magnify the greenhouse effect and bring about global climate change. These concerns have prompted law makers to consider public policies that limit or discourage production and consumption activities that contribute to emissions of greenhouse gases. One such policy is a carbon tax, a tax on fossil fuels based on their carbon content. Carbon dioxide emissions generally are proportional to carbon content; hence a carbon tax is effectively a tax proportional to the CO_2 emissions generated from the use of fossil fuels.[1]

The environmental benefits from carbon tax-induced reductions in CO_2 emissions need to be weighed against the economic costs that the tax would introduce. These costs include aggregate economic losses, which can be expressed in terms of such macroeconomic variables as GNP and aggregate consumption.[2] The distribution of these costs is also

---

[1] For a general discussion of the rationale for and potential effects of carbon taxes, see Goulder (1990), Lave (1991), and Poterba (1991).

[2] Several recent studies have employed simulation models to assess the aggregate costs of achieving reductions in CO_2 emissions through carbon taxes. See, for example, Goulder (1991a), Jorgenson and Wilcoxen (1990), and Manne and Richels (1990a, 1990b).

a critical policy consideration. It is important to know, in particular, the extent to which the economic burdens of the tax are concentrated in particular industries. It is also useful to assess the extent to which industries might shift the burden of the tax on to consumers. And it is important to understand the effects of the taxes on the ability of domestic firms to compete in the international marketplace. This paper examines these distributional effects.

Policy makers have several options in the design of a carbon tax. Important choices must be made regarding the application of the tax to internationally traded goods and the use of the revenues gained from the tax. In this paper we examine the importance of these different aspects of tax design to industry profits and to the potential of various industries to compete internationally.

To evaluate these effects, the paper applies a simulation model of the U.S. economy incorporating international trade. The model is general equilibrium in nature, enabling it to capture interactions across industries and between factor and product markets. The model also has a dynamic focus, with intertemporal decision making by firms and households, permitting an assessment of how the effects of taxes change over time as households and firms alter their supplies and demands.

The model is unique in combining three features critical to evaluating the inter-industry and international effects of carbon taxes. First, it contains a detailed treatment of U.S. taxes. The model addresses effects of taxes on investment incentives, equity values, industry profits, and savings decisions. Second, the model isolates major energy inputs and products, and incorporates important margins for substituting carbon-intensive products for other products when relative prices change. Such substitutions occur at both the industry and household level. Third, the model provides for international trade in both industry imputs and consumer goods. It considers how U.S. exports and imports of these goods change in response to changes in the relative prices of U.S. and foreign goods. This combination of features is especially useful for examining the implications of different types of carbon taxes for the distribution of the tax burden and "international competitiveness."

The rest of the paper is organized as follows. Section II discusses important issues related to the design of carbon taxes, indicating the potential significance to industries of the tax treatment of internationally traded goods and the use of tax revenues. Section III describes the simulation model used to evaluate the tax options, and Section IV presents and interprets results from the simulation experiments. Finally, Section V offers conclusions.

II. ISSUES IN TAX DESIGN

A. *Basic Issues*

It is generally recognized that, of the "greenhouse gases," carbon dioxide makes the largest contribution to the greenhouse effect. The U.S. Environmental Protection Agency (1989) estimates that increases in the atmospheric stock of CO_2 account for about half of the increase in radiative warming attributable to human activities. The CO_2 contribution (both relative and absolute) to such warming is expected to rise over the next century as CO_2 emissions grow. About 23 percent of global emissions of CO_2 stem from U.S. sources, and about 95 percent of U.S.-sourced emissions are generated by the combustion of fossil fuels—coal, oil, and natural gas.[3] The link between fossil fuel burning and CO_2 emissions is a rigid one: CO_2 emissions are an inevitable consequence of fossil fuel combustion. These considerations imply that any policy aimed at reducing the U.S. contribution to the greenhouse effect must confront the use of fossil fuels.

A carbon tax is one policy instrument for discouraging fossil fuel consumption. Such a tax can be justified on efficiency grounds. The environmental costs associated with fossil fuel use are largely external to the agent using the fuels.[4] Thus, in markets for fossil fuels, private costs may fail to capture all social costs.[5] Under these circumstances, the social value of reducing fossil fuel use may exceed the social costs of abatement. The carbon tax can be introduced as a corrective tax which, by internalizing costs that otherwise would be external to market decisions, promotes reduced fossil fuel use.

The externality here is associated with the quantity of CO_2 emissions.[6] The ratio of CO_2 emissions to carbon content of the fossil fuel is virtually the same for all uses of fossil fuels. Thus a tax whose value is based on the carbon content of a given fossil fuel is effectively a tax proportional to

---

[3] See World Resources Institute (1990, Table 24.2). Fossil fuel burning is the principal contributor to CO_2 emissions in most industrialized countries. The other important contributor is the burning of vegetation. This factor is significant in countries such as Brazil in which deforestation activities constitute a large portion of overall economic activity.

[4] The external costs from fossil fuel combustion include not only the environmental effects in terms of global climate change but also local air pollution. The former externalities are most relevant to CO_2 emissions and a carbon tax. The other externalities could provide an efficiency rationale for other taxes on fossil fuels.

[5] Whether private costs fall short of social costs depends on the extent of other pre-existing fuel taxes as well as the extent of other distortions in the economy.

[6] The external costs associated with a given emission of CO_2 need not be assumed to be constant through time. How the costs change depends on complex relationships between CO_2 emissions, CO_2 stocks, and the radiative warming. Peck and Teisberg (1991) discuss and evaluate these relationships.

CO_2 emissions.[7] Since the environmental damages depend on the quantity and not the value of carbon that is burned, efficiency considerations call for designing the carbon tax as a specific (or unit) tax, not as an *ad valorem* tax.

The value of the climate-change-related marginal damages associated with fossil fuel combustion is not known. The uncertainties here are vast.[8] Because the marginal damages are not known, no one can justifiably claim to know the magnitude of the "optimal" carbon tax.[9] One of the few "certainties" related to carbon taxes is that policy makers would need to make adjustments over time: If a carbon tax were to be introduced, it would be reasonable to alter the value of the tax rate in the future as more information became available.[10]

B. *Multilateral versus Unilateral Policies and the Treatment of Traded Goods*

A carbon tax would raise unit costs to producers of fossil fuels and to users of fossil-fuel-intensive products. If the tax were implemented worldwide at a uniform rate, for given industries the global distribution

---

[7] A complication arises from the fact that not all of the carbon in fossil fuels is burned. In the U.S., however, the share of carbon that is not combusted is quite small, less than 5% (see OECD/IEA, 1991). Carbon combustion can occur either through the burning of the fossil fuel or through the combustion of a derivative refined fuel. Carbon that is not combusted resides in "feedstocks" or nonfuel products made from fossil fuels. Because the carbon in feedstocks does not contribute to CO_2 (except, perhaps, when these products are incinerated after their useful economic life), there is little rationale for applying a carbon tax here. Thus if a carbon tax is introduced as a tax on fossil fuels, it would seem reasonable to accompany this tax with a rebate to users of feedstock carbon, with the rebate proportional to the carbon content in the feedstock.

[8] Pioneering work to assess the economic value of these benefits has been performed by Nordhaus (1990). The U.S. Environmental Protection Agency recently has begun to devote considerable resources to the study of this issue.

[9] Calculation of the optimal carbon tax rate generally will require other information in addition to the marginal external damages from fossil fuel burning. The literature on optimal taxation in the presence of externalities (see, for example, Sandmo, 1975) indicates that the optimal tax structure must consider not only the externality associated with a good's consumption but also the compensated elasticities of demand for the taxed good and other goods with respect to the price of the taxed good. If the social welfare function assigns different weights to the utilities of different individuals, then the optimal tax also depends on the distribution of the taxed good's consumption across different individuals. These considerations indicate that the optimal carbon tax generally will not involve the same tax per unit of carbon content for different fossil fuels.

[10] This suggests that carbon tax policies that preserve flexibility will often have an advantage over policies that remove future options. It also means that deciding on the appropriate carbon taxes today is fundamentally a problem of decision making under uncertainty, in which upside and downside risks of alternative options need to be considered. For one analysis of this issue, see Manne and Richels (1992).

of the changes in unit costs would be relatively uniform as well. The effects of the tax on the international competitive position of firms in given industries would be relatively small.[11] This is one attraction of multilateral carbon tax policies relative to unilateral initiatives. A multilateral approach also has the virtue of efficiency.[12] Global efficiency is served to the extent that marginal costs (including external costs) and benefits approach equality in all uses of fossil fuels in all regions of the globe. Uncoordinated, unilateral policies involving different tax rates would probably be less efficient.

Multilateral agreements are likely to be hard to achieve, however, for at least two reasons. First, the net benefits from multilateral carbon tax policies would be distributed very unevenly across countries. Large international transfers of funds would be necessary to make the distribution more even. Countries whose net transfers would be negative might be reluctant to support such schemes. Second, even if international transfers could be guaranteed, individual countries would often have incentives to spurn international agreements and act as free riders. Even though all countries could benefit from multilateral action in which all countries impose a carbon tax, a given country might do even better by free riding on an agreement reached by a number of other countries. The incentives to free ride are particularly strong for small countries who would enjoy only a small share of the environmental benefits related to their own emissions reductions.[13]

---

[11] There would still be some international competitiveness effects to the extent that firms in given industries differ across countries in their reliance on fossil fuels as inputs.

[12] It is important to recognize the sense in which "efficiency" is used here. If a multilateral carbon tax policy causes the marginal costs of emissions reductions to be equated throughout the globe, it will achieve efficiency in the sense that the global emissions reductions will have been attained at minimum cost. A broader notion of efficiency must confront the issue of whether the global reductions were too extensive or inadequate, that is, whether the global carbon tax policy was too severe or too weak. The fact that action has been taken multilaterally does not guarantee efficiency in this broader sense. A general equilibrium efficiency assessment would also consider production complementarities between taxed and untaxed goods, as indicated in Footnote 9.

This discussion of efficiency issues is not meant to suggest that global efficiency should be the only consideration in evaluating carbon tax policies. Distributional issues, for example, the distribution of costs of emissions reductions between richer and poorer countries, are critical as well.

[13] Recent experience suggests that this account of the incentives to small countries may be somewhat narrow. The countries that have already introduced policies resembling carbon taxes include Finland, Sweden, the Netherlands, and Germany. Except for Germany, these are small countries that, according to the present analysis, would have little to gain from such actions. Casual observation suggests that these actions have been taken in part to set an example for other nations to follow. Strong unilateral policies by small countries are rational to the extent that they increase the likelihood that other nations will follow suit.

As emphasized by Poterba (1991), the difficulties in reaching agreements for multilateral action make it reasonable for U.S. policy makers to contemplate unilateral policies even while considering potential multilateral initiatives. A given nation can improve its well being through a unilateral carbon tax, despite the fact that some (and perhaps most) of the environmental benefits from the policy will spill over to other countries.

C. Is A Carbon Tax That Safeguards International Competitiveness Administratively Feasible?

Unilateral policies present special challenges related to the impacts on industries significantly affected by international trade. Consider first an origin-based carbon tax, one that is levied only on domestic producers of fossil fuels. This tax could be imposed at the wellhead for oil and gas and at the mine mouth in the case of coal. By raising their costs, such a tax would put domestic producers at a significant disadvantage relative to their foreign competitors. An alternative is a destination-based tax. This tax applies to carbon that is consumed domestically. The destination (location of consumption) of the carbon, rather than the origin of its production, is the basis of this tax.

A destination-based tax can avoid cost disadvantages that the origin-based tax would impose on domestic producers in home and international markets. There are two potential ways to introduce a destination-based carbon tax. One way is by combining a tax on domestically produced fossil fuels with import levies and export subsidies for traded goods. Import levies and export subsidies would apply to traded fossil fuels according to their carbon content. The import levies would assure that imported fuels faced the same tax as domestically produced fuels consumed at home; the export subsidies would assure that domestically produced fuels devoted to the export market did not face the tax. To eliminate adverse effects on domestic producers of fossil-fuel-intensive products (for example, refined petroleum), the destination-based tax policy would need to include import levies and export subsidies for these products as well as for traded fossil fuels. Imported carbon-based products would need to be taxed according to their carbon content; this would avoid the potential cost disadvantage to domestic producers of carbon-based products. Similarly, exports of carbon-based products would receive a subsidy to offset the cost increase that the increase in fuel costs would otherwise bring about; this would help prevent a competitive disadvantage in the export market.

The second way to implement a destination-based tax appears more straightforward. Here the tax is implemented as one on all final goods purchased domestically, with the tax rate based on carbon content of the final goods. With the same tax rate per unit of carbon, this destination-based tax is equivalent to the first approach involving a fossil fuel tax plus import levies and export subsidies.

In designing a destination-based carbon tax, it helps to distinguish original and absorbed carbon. Original carbon is the carbon naturally contained in fossil fuels. The absorbed carbon of a unit of a given good is the amount of carbon contained in the fossil fuels used directly and indirectly in the manufacture of a unit of the good in question. The actual combustion of absorbed carbon may take place in the manufacturing process (as in the burning of coal to produce steel) or in the final use of a fossil-based product (as in the burning of home heating oil or other refined petroleum products).[14] If a tax were imposed on fossil fuels according to their (original) carbon content, the effect on production costs in a given industry will depend on the total carbon—original plus absorbed—in the goods manufactured by the industry. Appendix A describes in detail the method for evaluating the original and absorbed carbon content of produced goods and the relationship between carbon content and the costs of a carbon tax.

An attraction of the destination-based carbon tax is that it can avoid the direct adverse effects on international competitiveness that can result under the origin-based tax. At the same time, serious questions arise as to the administrative practicality of a full-fledged destination-based tax. Establishing carbon content can be especially difficult if production technologies differ across producers or change significantly with advances in knowledge or new economic conditions. If a destination-based tax were introduced as a domestic fossil fuel tax combined with import levies and export subsidies, the policy would require information on the carbon content of all traded goods. If introduced as a tax on carbon content of final goods consumed, the policy would require information on the carbon content of all final goods. Under either approach, the large numbers of goods involved and the difficulties of establishing carbon content call into question the feasibility of the policy.

The administrative problems are especially daunting under the approach that combines a fossil fuel tax with tariffs and subsidies for traded goods. The difficulties of ascertaining the carbon content of imported goods create scope for exploiting the uncertainties in imposing unjustifiably high tariff rates; this would abuse the environmental basis of the

---

[14] The amount of absorbed carbon in a given good includes the carbon content of fossil fuels used directly in production as well as the fossil fuels used indirectly in production, that is, the fossil fuels used to create other inputs in the production process. Thus, for example, the absorbed carbon in a unit of steel includes not only the carbon in the coal inputs to steel but also the carbon in the (fossil fuel) inputs to the inputs to steel.

policy and constitute protectionism under another name.[15] Moreover, under current arrangements under the General Agreements on Tariffs and Trade (GATT), the United States does not have the flexibility to levy additional, carbon-based tariffs on many products, since for many important products existing rates are already at the limits negotiated under the GATT.[16]

Do these problems make a destination-based policy impractical? The answer may depend on how fully one wishes to apply the destination principle. A full destination-based carbon tax may be prohibitively costly to administer, but a partial destination-based tax may still be practical. The practicality depends critically on the extensiveness of the set of goods with "significant" carbon content. If relatively few goods have significant carbon content, then it might make sense to design a destination-based tax that applies only to these goods (either through a fossil fuel tax plus import levies and subsidies or through a tax on consumption). A carbon tax that applies the destination principle to this limited set of goods might maintain the advantage of destination-based taxes in terms of preserving international competitiveness while remaining administratively feasible.

To begin an exploration of this issue, we present in Table 1 the overall carbon content of the industrial products and consumer goods contained in the model. This content was evaluated using the procedure described in Appendix A. Several findings emerge from the table. First, total embodied carbon content (per dollar of output) is highly concentrated among a few outputs: extracted fossil fuels, refined petroleum products, and electricity. The percentage cost increases from a given carbon tax are similarly concentrated. For consumer goods other than gasoline, a carbon tax would imply a very small cost increase compared with the increase for primary fuels.

The impact on unit costs is not the only relevant consideration in evaluating the impact of a carbon tax on competitiveness. It also is important to take account of the volume of trade. A domestic industry with a significant cost increase suffers no loss of international competitiveness if it is not involved in international trade; a domestic industry with a modest cost increase can suffer a significant loss if it faces stiff competi-

---

[15] Some might argue that the move from an origin-based to a destination-based carbon tax constitutes protectionism as well. It is difficult to define where protectionism begins.

[16] This is one issue within the broad class of issues concerning the relationship between international trade policies and international environmental concerns. Previous GATT negotiations largely have ignored environmental objectives, but trade negotiators are now beginning to recognize the need for integrating environmental goals with other important international trade objectives.

TABLE 1.
Distribution of Carbon Content and Tax Cost Across Industry and Consumer Good Categories of the Model.

	Carbon Content Per Dollar of Output (10^{-3} metric tons)			Pct. Cost Increase Per Dollar of Carbon Tax	1990 Imports ($ bill.)	Import-Weighted Cost Share	1990 Exports ($ bill.)	Export-Weighted Cost Share
	Original	Absorbed	Total					
A. Industry (and product)								
Agriculture and noncoal mining	0.00	0.06	0.06	0.004	3.7	0.02	21.0	0.32
Coal mining	22.88	5.96	28.84	2.878	0.1	0.69	5.5	64.48
Oil and gas extraction	5.56	0.65	6.21	0.620	71.9	76.34	0.0	0.00
Synthetic fuels	9.82	0.65	10.47	1.045	0.0	0.00	0.0	0.00
Petroleum refining	0.00	3.92	3.92	0.386	23.0	15.19	11.1	17.46
Electric utilities	0.00	2.77	2.77	0.267	0.7	0.32	0.1	0.12
Gas utilities	0.00	2.12	2.12	0.208	3.7	1.31	0.4	0.32
Construction	0.00	0.26	0.26	0.021	0.0	0.00	0.1	0.01
Metals and machinery	0.00	0.11	0.11	0.009	91.3	1.40	62.2	2.27
Motor vehicles (transportation equipment)	0.00	0.17	0.17	0.011	14.5	0.28	0.0	0.00
Miscellaneous manufacturing	0.00	0.22	0.22	0.017	138.7	4.13	131.3	9.32
Services (except electricity and gas)	0.00	0.20	0.20	0.018	10.1	0.31	78.2	5.70
Total					357.7	100.00	309.9	100.00

B. Consumer Good

Consumer Good								
Food	—	0.21	0.21	0.017	93.2	30.54	42.2	51.18
Alcohol	—	0.21	0.21	0.017	5.6	1.84	2.5	0.19
Tobacco	—	0.21	0.21	0.018	6.7	2.22	3.0	0.26
Utilities	—	1.74	1.74	0.170	0.2	0.52	4.0	0.08
Housing	—	0.03	0.03	0.002	0.0	0.00	0.9	0.00
Furnishing	—	0.23	0.23	0.019	15.4	5.58	7.5	1.67
Appliances	—	0.21	0.21	0.017	15.8	5.22	6.7	1.39
Clothing	—	0.21	0.21	0.018	39.0	12.94	17.2	8.85
Transportation	—	0.20	0.20	0.018	0.0	0.00	2.1	0.00
Motor Vehicles	—	0.19	0.19	0.015	63.5	18.15	37.3	26.91
Services	—	0.20	0.20	0.018	0.2	0.06	10.9	0.03
Financial Services	—	0.20	0.20	0.018	0.0	0.00	7.3	0.00
Recreation	—	0.39	0.39	0.035	23.4	15.63	11.2	6.96
Personal Care	—	0.21	0.21	0.018	15.7	5.17	5.8	1.20
Gasoline	—	2.69	2.69	0.265	0.0	0.00	2.0	0.00
Health	—	0.21	0.21	0.018	6.3	2.12	15.2	1.28
Education	—	0.20	0.20	0.018	0.0	0.00	2.4	0.00
Total					285.0	100.00	178.4	100.00

Notes: Carbon content calculated from 1986 U.S. input-output tables from the February 1991 *Survey of Current Business* and from data on fossil fuel carbon content provided by the Stanford University Energy Modeling Forum (Weyant, 1991). Technique for calculating original and absorbed carbon content and tax cost is described in Appendix A.

tion from imports or devotes a large share of its output to the export market. A rough way to account for the trade dimension is to weight the cost increase by the relative volume of imports or exports. The third-to-last and last columns of Table 1 provide the trade-weighted cost effects. These effects are somewhat more evenly distributed than the un-weighted effects. The carbon tax's impact on the metals and machinery industry, in particular, becomes much more significant given the large volumes of imports of such products. Still, for the majority of industries, the carbon tax impact is relatively insignificant. This suggests that a destination-based carbon tax which applies to a fairly limited number of carbon-based products would avert most of the adverse effects on inter-national competitiveness that could arise under an origin-based tax.

Using more disaggregated categories for industries and goods, one can obtain a sharper view of the distribution of carbon content and cost shares. Table 2 provides information similar to that in Table 1, but uses the more detailed industry categories contained in the input-output tables prepared by the Bureau of Economic Analysis of the U.S. Depart-ment of Commerce. The input-output tables distinguish eighty-five in-dustries; in Table 2 we list the twenty industries for which a given carbon tax would have the largest cost effect, where the effect here is the product of the percentage cost increase and the volume of imports or exports. The results in Table 2 largely conform to the results under the more aggregated industry categories in Table 1. The percentage cost increases from a given carbon tax are again highly concentrated among a few industries. The trade-weighted cost effects are somewhat more evenly distributed than the unweighted effects, but they are still concen-trated in a few industries. Twenty of the eighty-five industries account for over 87 percent of the import-weighted costs, and over 85 percent of the export-weighted costs.

Although the numbers in Tables 1 and 2 are informative, they do not fully convey the likely distribution and overall magnitude of interna-tional competitiveness effects from various carbon taxes. One reason is that the tables provide no information on potential behavioral responses to the carbon tax, specifically changes in demand patterns occasioned by changes in the relative prices of domestic and foreign intermediate and consumer goods. A closer assessment of these effects requires attention to policy-induced changes in trade volumes, domestic output levels, and market shares. In Section IV I assess these changes using a simulation model. It should also be kept in mind that aggregation of industries can mask important effects. An even more disaggregated analysis than that provided in Table 2 might reveal some new industries with substantial carbon content.

TABLE 2.
Distribution of Carbon Content and Tax Cost Across BEA Industry Classifications.

A. Industries Ranked by Import-Weighted Cost Share

BEA input-output classification	Carbon content per dollar of output (*)	Pct. cost increase per dollar of carbon tax	1986 imports ($ bill.)	Import-weighted cost share
08 Crude petroleum and natural gas	6.14	0.612	21.4	36.11
31 Petroleum refining and related industries	3.60	0.347	14.3	13.68
59 Motor vehicles and equipment	0.51	0.042	73.0	8.51
37 Primary iron and steel manufacturing	1.92	0.179	10.1	5.00
27 Chemicals and selected chemical products	1.34	0.119	10.3	3.37
18 Apparel	0.54	0.045	21.9	2.73
56 Radio, TV, and communication equipment	0.49	0.039	22.7	2.41
57 Electronic components and accessories	0.91	0.074	11.3	2.32
14 Food and kindred products	0.46	0.041	16.5	1.88
24 Paper and allied products, except container	0.94	0.084	8.1	1.86
68 Private electric, gas, water and sanitary	2.39	0.231	2.7	1.74
51 Office, computing and accounting machines	0.51	0.042	14.6	1.68
32 Rubber and miscellaneous plastics products	0.85	0.073	7.6	1.53
38 Primary nonferrous metals manufacturing	0.91	0.077	6.9	1.48
64 Miscellaneous manufacturing	0.42	0.035	14.4	1.40
36 Stone and clay products	0.86	0.079	4.0	0.86
16 Broad and narrow fabrics, yarn and others	1.05	0.089	3.3	0.80
34 Footwear and other leather products	0.43	0.035	7.9	0.75
42 Other fabricated metal products	0.58	0.050	5.5	0.75
63 Optical, opthalmic, and photographic equipment	0.47	0.039	6.2	0.66
Rest of the Sectors	0.50	0.042	222.4	10.49
Total			505.2	100.00

B. Industries Ranked by Export-Weighted Cost Share

BEA input-output classification	Carbon content per dollar of output (*)	Pct. cost increase per dollar of carbon tax	1986 exports ($ bill.)	Export-weighted cost share
07 Coal mining	27.54	2.734	3.2	37.68
31 Petroleum refining and related industries	3.60	0.347	6.5	9.64
27 Chemicals and selected chemicals products	1.34	0.119	15.0	7.56
69 Wholesale and retail trade	0.33	0.031	35.0	4.55
08 Crude petroleum and natural gas	6.14	0.612	1.5	3.99
59 Motor vehicles and equipment	0.51	0.042	16.9	3.04
51 Office, computing and accounting equipment	0.51	0.042	15.1	2.66
65 Transportation and warehousing	0.31	0.027	22.5	2.59
60 Aircraft and parts	0.35	0.030	19.3	2.48
28 Plastics and synthetic materials	1.49	0.127	4.5	2.42
57 Electronic components and accessories	0.91	0.074	7.5	2.38
14 Food and kindred products	0.46	0.041	12.1	2.13
24 Paper and allied products, except container	0.94	0.084	4.2	1.49
70 Finance and insurance	0.23	0.021	12.5	1.14
32 Rubber and miscellaneous plastics products	0.85	0.073	3.3	1.02
56 Radio, TV and communication equipment	0.49	0.039	5.3	0.87
37 Primary iron and steel manufacturing	1.92	0.179	1.1	0.86
45 Construction and mining machinery	0.49	0.041	4.8	0.85
38 Primary nonferrous metals manufacturing	0.91	0.077	2.6	0.85
49 General industrial machinery equipment	0.48	0.041	3.6	0.62
Rest of the Sectors	0.76	0.023	208.0	11.20
Total			404.6	100.00

*10^{-3} metric tons
Note: This table employs 1986 data, while Table 1 used 1986 data updated to 1990. The updating procedure generates some differences in carbon content across the two tables.

D. *Revenue Use*

Another important consideration in the design of a carbon tax is how its revenues might be used. One potential use of the revenues would be to finance reductions in other taxes. For example, the revenues could be used to pay for cuts in the corporate income tax. For many industries—particularly those with a relatively modest reliance on fossil fuel inputs—the corporate tax cut could neutralize all of the cost increase implied from the carbon tax.

Using the revenues to finance cuts in other taxes could generate general efficiency benefits as well as reduce the tax burden to particular industries. To the extent that carbon tax revenues are used to reduce other taxes that are highly distortionary, the cut in other taxes avoids tax distortions and leads to efficiency gains over and above the gains from more efficient use of fossil fuels.[17]

Thus, the use of carbon tax revenues, as well as the treatment of imports and exports, are important aspects of the design of a carbon tax. Alternative tax designs could lead to quite different outcomes in terms of the domestic and international distribution of the tax burden. In Section IV we examine numerically the industry effects of these alternative design options. The numerical results stem from the simulation model that I now briefly describe.

III. THE SIMULATION MODEL

I assess the effects of a carbon tax using a general equilibrium model of the United States, which incorporates international trade. Here I sketch out some main features of the model. Some details on the model's structure and parameters are offered in Appendix B. A more complete description is in Goulder (1991a, 1991b).

The model generates paths of equilibrium prices, outputs, and incomes for the U.S. economy under specified policy scenarios. These variables are calculated at yearly intervals beginning in the 1990 benchmark year and usually extending to the year 2065.

---

[17] Other possibilities are using the revenues to finance increases in federal government spending and using the revenues to reduce the federal debt. The latter alternative is equivalent to reducing future taxes, assuming that the government's debt cannot indefinitely grow faster than the interest rate (see, for example, Barro, 1979). Intuitively, reducing the government debt implies that future interest payments to service the debt will be lower. Hence, lower future taxes will be sufficient to meet the government's spending needs plus interest obligations.

A. The Production Sector

The model divides the U.S. production sector into 13 industries corresponding to the industry goods given in Table 1. The model also distinguishes the 17 consumer goods indicated in Table 1.

Each industry produces a distinct output (X), which is a function of inputs of labor (L), capital (K), an energy composite (E), and a materials composite (M), as well as the current level of investment (I):

$$X = f[g(L,K), h(E,M)] - \phi (I/K) \cdot I \tag{1}$$

The energy composite is made up of the outputs of the energy industries, while the materials composite is made up of the outputs of the other industries. Each of the individual inputs ($\bar{x}_1$, $\bar{x}_2$, etc.) making up E and M is, in turn, a composite of a domestic and foreign good from the given industry.[18]

In each industry, managers are assumed to serve stockholders by choosing inputs of labor, energy, and materials, and levels of investment to maximize the value of the firm. The optimal choices of labor and intermediate inputs minimize unit costs. The production system allows for substitutions among inputs at several levels. For example, when the relative price of a given energy input rises, producers generally reduce the relative intensity of use of that input, substituting other, less expensive energy inputs.[19] Similarly, when a domestic input rises in price relative to its foreign counterpart, producers tend to increase the use of the foreign input relative to the domestic input.

A distinguishing feature of the model is its attention to capital adjustment dynamics. In equation (1), $\phi(I/K) \cdot I$ represents capital adjustment (or installation) costs; these are an increasing function of the rate of investment.[20]

---

[18] The functions f, g, and h, and the aggregation functions for the composites E, M, and $\bar{x}_i$, are CES in form. Consumer goods are produced by combining outputs from the thirteen industries in given proportions.

[19] The model allows for complementarities in production, so that in some cases an increase in the price of a given input will, other things equal, reduce the quantity demanded of some other input.

[20] The cost function, ϕ, represents adjustment costs per unit of investment. This function is convex in I/K (see Appendix B) and expresses the notion that installing new capital necessitates a loss of current output, as existing inputs (K, L, E and M) that otherwise would be used to produce output are diverted to install the new capital. Here adjustment costs are internal to the firm. For a discussion of this and other adjustment cost specifications, see Mussa (1978). In choosing the optimal rate of investment, producers must balance the marginal costs of current investment (both the acquisition costs and installation

B. Special Features of the Oil-Gas and Synfuels Industries

1. Stock Effects in the Oil and Gas Industry. The production structure in the oil and gas industry is somewhat more complex than in other industries to account for the nonrenewable nature of oil and gas stocks. The production specification is:

$$X = \gamma(Z) \cdot f[g(L,K), h(E,M)] - \phi(I/K) \cdot I \tag{2}$$

where γ is a decreasing function of Z, the amount of cumulative extraction (or output) of oil and gas up to the beginning of the current period. The presence of $\gamma(Z)$ in the production function distinguishes the oil and gas industry from other industries. The function γ is decreasing in Z. This captures the fact that as Z rises (or, equivalently, as reserves are depleted), it becomes increasingly difficult to extract oil and gas resources, so that greater quantities of K, L, E, and M are required to achieve any given level of extraction (output). Increasing production costs ultimately induce oil and gas producers to shut down their operations.[21]

2. Emergence of a Backstop Technology. The model incorporates a synthetic fuel, shale oil, as a backstop resource, a perfect substitute for oil and gas. The parameters of the synfuels production function are chosen so that, with real prices of inputs at 1990 levels, it costs $50 to produce the quantity of synfuels with an energy content equivalent to that of a barrel of oil. For comparison, the 1990 price of a barrel of oil was just under $24. As in other industries, in the synfuels industry producers choose input and investment levels to maximize the equity value of the firm. There is, however, one difference. The technology for producing synthetic fuels on a commercial scale is assumed to become known only in the year 2010. Thus, capital formation in the synfuels industry cannot begin until the year 2010. The rate of capital formation and the level of production of synfuels depend directly on the price of oil and gas.

All domestic prices in the model are endogenous, except for the domestic price of oil and gas. The latter is given by the exogenous world price of oil and gas plus whatever oil tariff may apply. This world price is specified as $24 per barrel in 1990 and as rising in real terms by $6.50 per

---

costs of new capital) with the marginal benefits (the stream of increased dividends made possible by a higher future capital stock).

[21] For a detailed presentation of the economic considerations involved, see Goulder (1991b).

decade.[22] At any given point in time, the supply of imported oil and gas is taken to be perfectly elastic at the given world price. So long as imports are the marginal source of supply to the domestic economy, domestic producers of oil and gas receive the world price (adjusted for tariffs or taxes) for their own output. But rising oil and gas prices stimulate investment in synfuels. Eventually, synfuels production plus domestic oil and gas supply together satisfy all of domestic demand. Synfuels then become the marginal source of supply, and the cost of synfuels production rather than the world oil price dictates the domestic price of fuels.[23]

The gradual replacement of conventional oil and gas fuels by synthetic fuels is significant in a study of the carbon tax because the carbon content of synthetic fuels differs from that of oil and gas. The transition from conventional oil and gas to synfuels tends to make the economy more carbon-intensive and contributes to a gradual increase in the carbon tax base.[24]

C. *The Household and Government Sectors*

Consumption, labor supply, and saving result from the decisions of an infinitely lived representative household that maximizes intertemporal utility, subject to the constraint that the present value of the consumption stream not exceed the value of the household's overall economic resources. In each period, overall consumption expenditure is allocated across the seventeen types of consumer goods. In most cases, each type includes both domestically produced and foreign-made products. Changes in relative prices cause households to substitute between domestic and foreign goods of a given type.

The government collects taxes, issues debt, and purchases goods and services (outputs of the thirteen industries). The wide array of tax instruments in the model includes carbon taxes, output taxes, the corporate income tax, property taxes, sales taxes, and taxes on individual labor and capital income.

In the policy experiments in this paper, we require that government

---

[22] These price assumptions match reference case assumptions of the Energy Modeling Forum (see Weyant, 1991) at Stanford University.

[23] For details, see Goulder (1991a).

[24] The carbon content per unit of energy from synthetic fuels is about 75 percent greater than that of an equivalent energy unit of oil or gas. Another important factor promoting the trend toward increasing carbon intensity is the substitution of coal for oil and gas. Per unit of energy, coal has 21 percent more carbon than oil and 76 percent more carbon than natural gas. Over time, coal is increasingly substituted for oil and gas because (absent policy changes) coal prices are expected to rise more slowly than prices of oil and gas. This reflects the fact that coal reserves are vastly more abundant than those of oil and gas.

spending and the government deficit follow the same path as in the baseline (status quo) simulation. To meet its cash flow requirements, the government must obtain tax revenues equal to the given overall government spending level minus the given government deficit. Depending on the policy experiment desired, either lump-sum tax adjustments or changes in personal or corporate tax rates are applied to assure that the required total tax revenues are generated.

D. Equilibrium and Growth

The solution of the model is a general equilibrium in which supplies and demands balance in all markets at each period of time. Thus the solution requires that supply equal demand for labor inputs and for all produced goods,[25] that firms' demands for loanable funds equal the aggregate supply by households, and that the government's tax revenues equal its spending less the current deficit. These conditions are met through adjustments in output prices, in the market interest rate, and in lump-sum taxes or tax rates.[26]

Economic growth reflects the growth of capital stocks and of potential labor resources. The growth of capital stocks stems from endogenous saving and investment behavior. Potential labor resources are specified as increasing at a constant rate. In each period, potential labor divides between hours worked and leisure time in accordance with utility-maximizing household decisions.

E. Data and Parameters

Complete data documentation for model is provided in Cruz and Goulder (1991). In the present subsection I indicate the sources for some important data and parameters. The data stem from several sources. Industry input and output flows (used to establish production function share parameters) were obtained from 1986 input-output tables published in the February 1991 *Survey of Current Business*. These tables were also the source for consumption, investment, government spending, import and export values by industry. The year 1990 is the initial period for the simulations of this paper. To obtain 1990 values, we scaled up the

---

[25] Because oil and gas and synfuels are perfect substitutes, they generate a single supply-demand condition.

[26] When oil and gas imports are the marginal source of supply for the domestic economy, the quantity of these imports is an equilibrating variable, and the oil and gas price is exogenous. Once synfuels become the marginal source of supply (that is, once synfuels drive oil and gas imports to zero), the synfuels price becomes an equilibrating variable. Since agents are forward-looking, equilibrium in each period depends not only on current prices and taxes but on future magnitudes as well.

1986 data using information for major industry groups in the 1991 *Economic Report of the President*. For the oil and gas, coal, and petroleum refining industries, further adjustments were made to make the relative 1990 values correspond closely to relative values projected for 1988 by the OECD (see OECD/IEA, 1990). The carbon content of different fossil fuels was calculated by multiplying the amount of carbon per unit of heat content times the heat content per unit of fuel. The information used here was taken from the *1989 Annual Energy Outlook* published by the U.S. Department of Energy.

Elasticities of substitution for industry production functions were obtained by transforming translog production function parameters estimated by Dale Jorgenson and Peter Wilcoxen. Elasticities of substitution between domestic and foreign goods were obtained by aggregating estimates from Shiells, Stern, and Deardorff (1986).

In the oil and gas industry, the function $\gamma(Z)$ relates output to cumulative extraction, Z. Although most of the model's parameters derive from econometric estimates, in the case of the γ function existing estimates were not available and it was not possible to obtain information sufficient to generate new estimates. A rough calibration method was employed to generate parameters of the $\gamma(Z)$ function: parameters were chosen so that, given current reserves and projected prices of oil and gas, it would cease to be economic to invest in new domestic oil and gas wells after the year 2030. This is in keeping with the projections of Masters et al. (1987). It should be recognized that because this calibration procedure makes use of projections about future costs and reserves rather than observed magnitudes, the uncertainty bands on the chosen parameters are especially wide.

Appendix B indicates functional forms and lists parameter values for the production and household sectors.

IV. SIMULATION RESULTS

A. *The Baseline*

The baseline is the projected economic path under the assumption of no change in policy. This is a reference path for evaluating the effects of alternative carbon taxes. Values under the baseline scenario are given in Table 3 and Figure 1.

In the baseline scenario, the exogenously specified increases in world oil and gas prices translate into rising relative prices of commodities that are especially oil and gas intensive, most notably refined petroleum products and natural gas utilities. Consumption of oil and gas increases more slowly than that of coal. The depletion of domestic oil and gas

TABLE 3.
Baseline Values.

Industry	Year	Output price	Domestic output	Net profits	Net investment
Coal mining					
	1990	1.000	37.6	1.0	1.4
	2000	0.998	46.7	1.2	1.8
	2020	0.992	71.3	1.9	2.7
Oil and gas extraction					
	1990	1.000	126.4	33.4	3.9
	2000	1.271	101.5	34.6	3.2
	2020	1.812	62.8	33.4	−3.5
Synthetic fuels					
	1990	1.000	0.0	0.0	0.0
	2000	1.271	0.0	0.0	0.0
	2020	1.812	5.2	−1.0	23.8
Petroleum refining					
	1990	1.000	200.3	15.3	15.8
	2000	1.152	208.1	17.0	18.4
	2020	1.444	247.5	23.4	25.7
Electric utilities					
	1990	1.000	144.5	24.7	45.1
	2000	1.008	175.0	29.3	55.2
	2020	1.022	256.5	42.5	82.5
Gas utilities					
	1990	1.002	135.6	22.0	38.9
	2000	1.074	158.5	26.2	47.7
	2020	1.204	218.5	38.6	71.2
Nonenergy manufacturing					
	1990	1.000	4,919.2	742.5	771.0
	2000	0.993	6,034.4	893.7	948.9
	2020	0.980	9,060.8	1,321.7	1,422.4
Nonenergy services					
	1990	0.999	4,200.6	600.4	700.7
	2000	0.989	5,120.5	706.4	853.9
	2020	0.970	7,597.9	1,010.4	1,266.8
Total					
	1990	1.000	9,764.2	1,439.4	1,576.8
	2000	1.000	11,844.8	1,708.3	1,929.0
	2020	1.000	17,520.5	2,470.8	2,891.5

Output, profits, and investment are in billions of 1990 dollars. Prices are relative to the given year's producer price index.

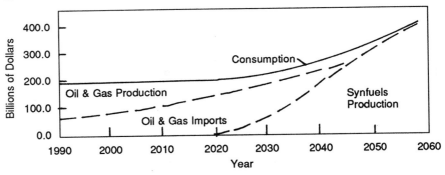

a.

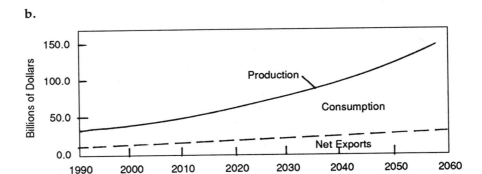

b.

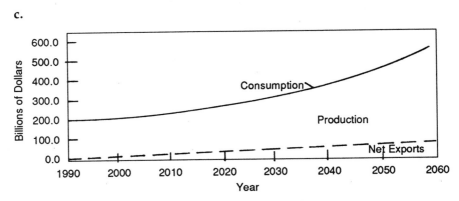

c.

FIGURE 1. *Baseline Fuel Production and Consumption (evaluated at 1990 prices).* **a.** *oil and gas and synfuel;* **b.** *coal;* **c.** *refined petroleum products.*

reserves implies rising unit costs, relatively low gross investment (zero by 2031), and declining output in the domestic oil and gas industry. At the same time, rising oil and gas prices stimulate investment in synthetic fuels. Such fuels entirely eliminate oil and gas imports before the middle of the next century.

B. A Carbon Tax: General Results

Here we examine the consequences of alternative carbon taxes. In all experiments, the carbon tax rate is $25 (in 1990 dollars) per metric ton of carbon at all points in time beginning with the first simulation period (1990). In our first, "central case" experiment, the tax is applied on a partial destination basis: There is a tax on all domestically produced fossil fuels, augmented by a tax on imported fossil fuels and a subsidy for exported fossil fuels. This is not a fully destination-based tax because it does not apply to cover imported fossil-fuel-based products and does not exempt exported fossil-fuel-based products (as discussed in Section II). In this experiment, the path of total revenue from the carbon tax and other pre-existing taxes is kept the same as in the baseline (no-policy-change) case through lump-sum reductions in individual income taxes.

1. Price and Output Effects.

Table 4 shows the effects of this tax across industries. To avoid overwhelming the reader with numbers, I have aggregated results for the construction, metals and machinery, motor vehicles, and miscellaneous manufacturing industries into a single "nonenergy manufacturing" category; results for the nonresidential and residential services industries are aggregated into a single "nonenergy services" category.

The coal mining industry feels the greatest impact from the carbon tax. This is in keeping with the fact that coal is the most carbon-intensive of fossil fuels. At unchanged pre-tax prices, the $25 per ton carbon tax would raise the price of coal by 72.0 percent.[27] Table 4 shows that, on impact, the price of coal rises by 64.1 percent, indicating that consumers bear approximately three-fourths of the tax burden. Initially, coal output falls by approximately 37 percent. This substantial reduction allows the coal market to clear at significantly higher coal prices (shifting some of the tax burden on to consumers). Over the

---

[27] Table 1 shows that at unchanged pretax prices, the cost increase is 2.878 percent per dollar of tax. Multiplying this number times twenty-five yields the figure of 72.0 percent. Note that this increase includes both the direct cost effect from the tax on coal output plus the effect from higher prices of the absorbed carbon used to produce coal.

TABLE 4.
Industry Effects of a $25 per Ton Carbon Tax
(percentages changes from baseline path).

Industry	Year	Output price	Domestic output	Net profits	Net investment
Coal mining					
	1990	64.1	−37.1	−41.1	−26.2
	2000	66.3	−39.0	−40.4	−33.3
	2020	68.5	−40.6	−38.2	−38.6
Oil and gas extraction					
	1990	13.9	−1.4	−1.9	1.1
	2000	10.9	−0.9	−2.3	−0.1
	2020	7.7	−0.5	−2.5	−0.6
Synthetic fuels					
	1990	—	—	—	—
	2000	—	—	—	—
	2020	7.7	−41.9	−47.1	−39.1
Petroleum refining					
	1990	7.2	−8.9	−6.0	−3.3
	2000	6.3	−7.2	−4.1	−2.5
	2020	4.8	−5.1	−2.4	−1.7
Electric utilities					
	1990	4.0	−3.3	−1.3	−0.6
	2000	4.3	−3.6	−1.4	−0.8
	2020	4.4	−4.0	−1.5	−1.1
Gas utilities					
	1990	4.6	−2.8	0.6	0.2
	2000	3.5	−2.3	0.1	0.1
	2020	2.4	−1.9	−0.5	−0.0
Nonenergy manufacturing					
	1990	−0.8	−0.3	−1.3	−0.3
	2000	−0.8	−0.4	−1.4	−0.5
	2020	−0.8	−0.6	−1.5	−0.4
Nonenergy services					
	1990	−0.7	−0.4	−1.1	−0.3
	2000	−0.7	−0.5	−1.5	−0.5
	2020	−0.7	−0.6	−1.7	−0.6
Total					
	1990		−0.7	−1.0	−0.3
	2000		−0.9	−1.1	−0.5
	2020		−1.2	−1.2	−0.9

$25 per ton carbon tax on partial destination basis with lump-sum revenue replacement.

longer term, producers adjust further to the policy shock and reduce coal output by a larger percentage (41 percent). The larger reduction in coal output helps bring about the larger percentage increase in coal prices (68.5 percent) in the long run.

Prices also rise substantially in the oil and gas industry. The price rises by 13.9 percent initially (1990) and by 7.7 percent in 2020. The percentage increase is smaller in the long run because the constant real tax is a continuously declining percentage of the rising world oil price. The effects on the synfuels industry are dramatic. These results should be taken as suggestive. They depend upon best guesses about input requirements and adjustment costs for a technology that is still undergoing fundamental changes. The results in Table 4 suggest that a carbon tax would significantly retard the rate of introduction of synfuels: In the year 2020, synfuels output would be 42 percent below the level that it would achieve in that year if there were no carbon tax. In the baseline simulation, synfuels account for about 75 percent of consumption of oil and gas plus synfuels in the year 2040; under the carbon tax, synfuels only account for 57 percent of consumption in that year. The price increase is also significant in the petroleum refining industry, which makes intensive use of oil and gas.

The carbon tax causes some prices to fall in real (or relative) terms. This is the case for the nonenergy manufacturing and services industries, which depend relatively little on fossil fuels for inputs. It should be noted that these are relative price changes. Whether absolute prices would rise in these (and other) industries depends on monetary policy and other factors that are not incorporated in the model.

2. Effects on Profits and Investment. The carbon tax implies a reduction in profits in all industries except in the gas utilities industry, which provides a substitute for electric utilities. (Even the gas utilities industry suffers a loss of profits after 2010.) The percentage reductions in profits differ significantly across industries. Fossil fuel producers generally suffer the largest losses. Interestingly, the effects on profits are minor in the oil and gas industry; we address this issue in subsection C. There are significant reductions in profits in the petroleum refining and electric utilities industries, which make intensive use of fossil fuels. The long-run reductions in profits are small in the gas utilities industry and the nonenergy industries, which depend relatively little on fossil fuels.

In general, changes in investment correspond to anticipated changes in profits. By far the largest reductions in investment occur in the coal mining industry, where investment declines by about 26 percent initially and by 39 percent in 2020.

C. Origin- vs. Destination-Based Taxes

1. Effects on Industry Performance.

Table 5 compares results under alternative carbon tax designs. The table considers an origin-based and full destination-based tax as well as the partial destination-based tax just discussed.

Consider first the differences between results for an origin-based tax and for a partial destination-based tax. The differences are dramatic for the domestic oil and gas industry. The former policy does not tax imported oil, while the latter does. The market price that domestic producers receive for oil is the world price gross of any oil tariff. Under the origin-based tax, there is no tariff-induced increase in this market price to offset the tax that must be paid on domestically produced oil. Hence domestic oil production and profits are substantially lower under the origin-based tax. In contrast, under the partial destination-based tax, the tariff on imported oil raises the consumer price of oil by enough to offset the tax on domestically produced oil. The producer price is largely unaffected by the carbon tax. Although the higher consumer price reduces overall demands for oil, domestic producers are largely unaffected because imports, not domestically produced oil, represent the marginal source of supply.

While the oil and gas industry fares much better under the partial destination-based tax, the opposite is true for the petroleum refining industry. This is the case because the partial destination-based tax raises the market price of crude oil, the most important input to this industry.[28] For similar reasons, in the electric utilities, nonenergy manufacturing, and nonenergy services industries profits are lower under the partial destination-based tax than under the origin-based tax.

The move from a partial to full destination-based carbon tax[29] has a profound effect on profits in petroleum refining. The latter tax would eliminate much of the direct cost disadvantage that a carbon tax would otherwise inflict on domestic refiners. While the partial destination-based carbon reduces profits to domestic refiners by about 6 percent in the short run, the full destination-based tax enables these producers to continue to supply the export market, and there is no significant effect on profits.

---

[28] Our analysis assumes that oil and gas production and petroleum refining are carried out by separate enterprises. The analysis for a vertically integrated firm involved in both activities would be considerably more complex.

[29] We model the full destination-based tax as a tax on domestic fossil fuels combined with import levies and export subsidies for traded fuels and fossil-fuel-based products. As discussed in Section II, it would be equivalent to implement this policy as a tax on domestic consumption of final goods, with the tax rate based on carbon content.

An important result from Table 5 is that the move from a partial to a full destination-based tax has minimal effect on production and profits by industries other than petroleum refining. This is in keeping with the initial insights that could be gleaned from Table 1. This suggests that a carbon tax that applies the destination principle to a selected set of products (imported fossil fuels, imported refined products, and perhaps a few others) might avoid nearly all of the significant adverse implications for international competitiveness while remaining administratively feasible.

2. Implications of Tax Basis for Emissions.   One argument for a destination-based rather than origin-based carbon tax is that the former is more effective in reducing U.S. demands for fossil fuels and curtailing global carbon emissions. To the extent that an origin-based carbon tax leads producers and consumers to substitute (now cheaper) imports for domestically produced fuels and fossil-fuel-based products, the magnitude of the reduction in domestic consumption of (demands for) carbon-based goods would be smaller and the benefit to the global environment would be reduced. A destination-based tax reduces options for such substitution.

Figure 2 provides information indicating the extent to which this issue may be important. Consider the effects in the year 2000. Under the origin-based tax, U.S. firms reduce production of emissions by 0.60 billion metric tons (Figure 2b), a reduction of about 37 percent from the corresponding year in the baseline. Emissions consumption falls by only 0.26 billion tons, however. This means that the reduction in production is offset by .34 billion in increased "net imports" of emissions.

The destination-based taxes are more effective in reducing emissions demands. As Figure 2a indicates, the reduction in demands is 40 to 45 percent greater under destination-based taxes than under the origin-based tax.[30] At the same time, there is relatively little difference between the partial and full destination-based policies in terms of emissions production and consumption. Although the full destination-based tax expands the range of imports which face the carbon tax, it appears that the volume of trade in these imports and the carbon content of these goods together are not sufficient to have a substantial impact on total emissions consumption. It may be vitally important to some industries (for example, petroleum refining) to expand the carbon tax to cover not only imported fuels but fossil fuel-based products as well; much may be at stake in terms of the international competitiveness of particular indus-

---

[30] It may be noted that there is a greater cutback in consumption even though U.S. production of emissions is higher under the destination-based policies.

TABLE 5.
Significance of Tax Basis for Profits and International Trade (percentage changes from baseline).

	1 Coal mining		2 Oil and gas extraction		3 Synthetic fuels		4 Petroleum refining		5 Electric utilities		6 Gas utilities		7 Nonenergy manufacturing		8 Nonenergy services	
	1990	2020	1990	2020	1990	2020	1990	2020	1990	2020	1990	2020	1990	2020	1990	2020
1. Origin-Based Tax																
Output Price	60.8	68.2	0.0	0.1	—	0.1	-0.1	-0.1	2.6	4.1	-0.2	-0.1	-0.1	-0.4	-0.4	-0.3
Domestic Production	-51.4	-53.7	-12.9	-1.3	—	-65.8	0.1	-0.3	-2.4	-3.8	0.0	-0.2	0.0	-0.5	-0.1	-0.5
Domestic Construction	-40.8	-43.0	-1.1	-0.8	—	-65.8	-0.1	-0.3	-2.4	-3.8	0.0	-0.2	-0.2	-0.7	-0.2	-0.5
Exports	-75.5	-78.9	0.0	0.0	—	0.0	1.9	-0.3	-2.4	-4.4	20.0	-2.3	2.5	0.8	2.2	-0.5
Imports	89.1	105.1	21.9	1.9	—	0.0	-0.1	-0.4	-2.4	-3.8	0.0	2.9	-0.6	-0.9	-0.2	-0.5
Profits	-66.2	-59.3	-27.8	-11.0	—	-70.6	0.1	-0.5	-2.2	-2.1	-0.1	-0.6	-0.1	-0.9	-0.4	-1.1

2. Partial Destination-Based Tax

Output Price	64.1	68.6	13.9	7.7	—	7.7	7.2	4.8	4.0	4.4	4.5	2.4	-0.7	-0.8	-0.6	-0.7
Domestic Production	-37.1	-40.6	-1.3	-0.5	—	-41.9	-8.9	-5.1	-3.3	-4.0	-2.8	-1.9	-0.3	-0.6	-0.3	-0.6
Domestic Construction	-41.5	-43.6	-11.7	-5.9	—	-41.9	-3.9	-3.0	-3.2	-4.0	-2.6	-1.8	-0.2	-0.6	-0.2	-0.6
Exports	-26.0	-33.1	0.0	0.0	—	0.0	-31.2	-17.0	-51.6	-52.0	-2.8	-1.9	-1.6	-0.6	-2.7	-0.6
Imports	-29.8	-32.3	-32.1	-8.4	—	0.0	12.8	8.2	-3.2	-3.8	0.9	4.4	-1.0	-0.8	-0.2	-0.6
Profits	-41.1	-38.2	-1.9	-2.5	—	-47.1	-6.0	-2.4	-1.3	-1.5	0.6	-0.5	-1.3	-1.5	-1.1	-1.7

3. Full Destination-Based Tax

Output Price	64.2	68.6	13.9	7.7	—	7.7	8.3	4.8	4.6	4.6	5.0	2.5	-0.8	-0.8	-0.6	-0.7
Domestic Production	-37.2	-40.8	-1.4	-0.5	—	-41.2	-5.3	-3.6	-3.4	-3.9	-2.6	-1.6	-0.3	-0.7	-0.4	-0.6
Domestic Construction	-41.2	-43.4	-8.9	-4.8	—	-41.2	-5.8	-4.2	-3.4	-3.9	-2.5	-1.7	-0.2	-0.6	-0.3	-0.6
Exports	-27.3	-34.1	0.0	0.0	—	0.0	-1.8	-1.2	-3.4	-3.9	-2.6	-3.0	-2.0	-1.5	-2.7	-0.6
Imports	-29.5	-32.1	-23.7	-6.9	—	0.0	-6.6	-7.1	-3.4	-3.9	-2.5	-1.6	-0.4	-0.6	-0.3	-0.6
Profits	-40.8	-38.1	-1.9	-0.7	—	-46.4	0.1	-0.5	-0.5	-1.0	1.4	-0.1	-1.5	-1.6	-1.0	-1.7

a.

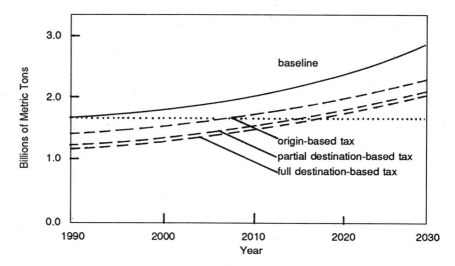

b.

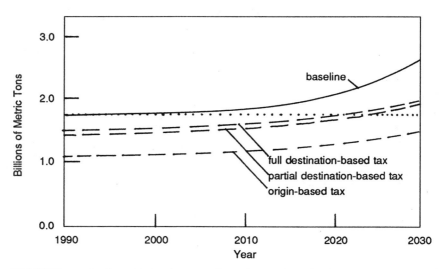

FIGURE 2. *Carbon Emissions under Alternative Carbon Taxes.* **a.** *consumption (emissions demanded);* **b.** *production (emissions supplied).*

tries. But in terms of U.S. emissions consumption, it would appear that much less hangs in the balance.

D. Implications of Alternative Revenue Uses

Table 6 compares results under different specifications for the use of the tax revenues. All policy experiments involve the partial destination-based tax. The first experiment is the same one as considered in subsection A, and involves lump-sum replacement of the tax revenues. In the second experiment, additional revenues from the tax are returned through reductions in the statutory corporate income tax rate. In the last experiment, the additional revenues are returned through reductions in the marginal tax rates applied to individual labor and capital income.[31]

The profits performance of all industries is better, but only slightly better, under the latter two policies than under lump-sum revenue replacement. Lowering corporate or individual tax rates has the attraction of reducing the efficiency losses that these distortionary taxes generate. In contrast, returning revenues in lump-sum fashion yields no direct efficiency benefit. The more favorable profits performance under the corporate and personal tax reduction cases is consistent with the improvement in economic efficiency.

Although the picture improves when revenues finance reductions in distortionary taxes, none of these policies succeeds in eliminating the burden (in terms of lost profits) to all industries. Fossil fuel producers, in particular, still experience lost profits, although the losses are smaller. These results suggest that sagacious use of tax revenues would not prevent at least some industries from adverse effects from a carbon tax. This conclusion is reinforced by the aggregate efficiency results reported in the next subsection.

E. Some Aggregate Results

Table 7 displays GNP and welfare effects of the various tax options we have considered. Numbers in parentheses are percentage changes in GNP relative to the baseline simulation.

In all the cases considered, the carbon tax causes GNP to fall. The GNP falls by considerably more under the destination-based carbon taxes than under the origin-based tax. This is in keeping with the fact that the United States is a net importer of emissions: There are more emissions associated with its consumption than with its production. The destination-based tax

---

[31] This experiment involves proportionate reductions in the marginal rates on labor income, dividend and interest income, and capital gains income for the representative household. The benchmark marginal rates are weighted averages of rates faced by U.S. households, with weights based on income levels.

TABLE 6.
Effects of a Carbon Tax under Alternative Specifications for Revenue Use.

	1 Coal mining		2 Oil & Gas extraction		3 Synthetic fuels		4 Petroleum refining		5 Electric utilities		6 Gas utilities		7 Nonenergy manufacturing		8 Nonenergy services	
	1990	2020	1990	2020	1990	2020	1990	2020	1990	2020	1990	2020	1990	2020	1990	2020
1. Lump-Sum Tax Replacement																
Domestic Production	-37.1	-40.6	-1.4	-0.5	.	-41.9	-8.9	-5.1	-3.3	-4.0	-2.8	-1.9	-0.3	-0.6	-0.4	-0.6
Net Investment	-26.2	-38.6	1.1	-0.6	.	-39.1	-3.3	-1.7	-0.6	-1.1	0.2	-0.1	-0.3	-0.4	-0.3	-0.6
Net Profits	-41.1	-38.2	-1.9	-0.8	.	-47.1	-6.1	-2.4	-1.3	-1.5	0.6	-0.5	-1.3	-1.5	-1.1	-1.7
2. Corporate Income Tax Replacement																
Domestic Production	-37.1	-40.5	-1.4	-0.6	.	-41.9	-8.7	-5.0	-3.3	-3.9	-2.8	-1.8	-0.3	-0.4	-0.4	-0.5
Net Investment	-26.0	-38.4	1.0	-0.6	.	-38.8	-3.2	-1.3	-0.6	-1.0	0.2	0.1	-0.1	0.1	-0.3	-0.4
Net Profits	-41.0	-37.9	-1.5	-0.2	.	-28.0	-5.7	-2.0	-1.1	-1.2	0.7	-0.1	-0.9	-1.0	-0.7	-1.3
3. Personal Income Tax Replacement																
Domestic Production	-37.1	-40.5	-1.4	-0.5	.	-41.9	-8.7	-5.0	-3.3	-3.9	-2.8	-1.8	-0.3	-0.5	-0.4	-0.5
Net Investment	-26.1	-38.5	1.1	-0.5	.	-39.1	-3.2	-1.5	-0.5	-1.1	0.3	0.0	-0.2	-0.2	-0.2	-0.5
Net Profits	-41.0	-38.0	-1.6	-0.6	.	-37.8	-6.0	-2.1	-1.2	-1.3	0.6	-0.4	-1.0	-1.1	-0.9	-1.5

TABLE 7.
Effects on GNP and Welfare.

| | Real GNP | | | Welfare |
	1990	2000	2020	Change
Baseline:	5603.9	6773.1	9876.0	
Carbon Tax:				
Origin Basis	5581.6	6739.6	9800.5	−0.633
	(−0.40)	(−0.49)	(−0.76)	
Partial Destination Basis	5566.5	6715.9	9769.1	−0.712
(Lump-Sum Replacement)	(−0.67)	(−0.84)	(−1.08)	
Full Destination Basis	5563.5	6712.3	9763.6	−0.726
	(−0.72)	(−0.90)	(−1.14)	
Partial Destination Basis,	5567.5	6725.7	9800.9	−0.482
Corporate Tax Replacement	(−0.65)	(−0.70)	(−0.76)	
Partial Destination Basis,	5568.0	6723.7	9793.0	−0.536
Personal Tax Replacement	(−0.64)	(−0.73)	(−0.84)	

Note: The upper number in each pair of GNP figures is GNP in billions of 1990 dollars. The lower number is the percentage change from the baseline. The welfare change is the equivalent variation as a percentage of baseline financial wealth.

applies to emissions consumption, the origin-based tax to production. The destination-based tax therefore has a larger base, which contributes to the larger GNP impact.[32]

When carbon tax revenues are used to reduce other distortionary taxes, the GNP effects are still negative, but smaller in absolute value than under the lump-sum tax case.

In all simulations, the percentage losses of GNP are greater in the long run than in the short run. This is in keeping with the gradual shift of the economy away from oil and gas and toward coal and synfuels, which are more carbon-intensive and yield a larger tax base.[33]

Welfare changes are similar to the changes in GNP. The measure of welfare change is the equivalent variation as a percentage of baseline wealth.[34] Even when carbon tax revenues finance cuts in distortionary

[32] The model is somewhat biased toward pessimism in its assessment of GNP losses from the destination-based taxes. The model assumes the United States has no monopsony power to influence world prices of the goods it imports. If reduced imports caused world (pre-tariff) import prices to fall, the magnitude of the adverse effects on U.S. GNP would be smaller.

[33] On impact, the carbon tax induces substitutions of oil and gas for coal, which is more carbon-intensive and more highly taxed. Following this initial effect, coal use rises more quickly than oil and gas use. This reflects rising real world prices of oil and gas and relatively steady real prices of coal.

[34] Wealth is the present value of after-tax labor and capital income over an infinite time horizon.

taxes, the welfare changes are negative. The consistently negative effects on GNP and welfare are in keeping with the effects on industry profits noted earlier.

The negative welfare numbers for the last two policies given in the table suggest that carbon taxes cannot be justified on narrow efficiency grounds; they indicate that these taxes tend to cause greater distortions than the distortionary taxes they might partly replace.[35] It should be kept in mind that these welfare figures disregard the environmental benefits from reduced carbon emissions. These results indicate that one needs to invoke these environmental benefits to justify carbon tax policies.

F. Sensitivity Analysis

Here I explore the extent to which the distribution of industry burdens under a carbon tax might be sensitive to the values of important parameters. I concentrate on the distribution of industry burdens under the original simulation described under IV.A.: The partial destination-based carbon tax with revenues returned to the economy in lump-sum fashion.

I consider the implications of changes in the values of (1) elasticities of substitution between domestically produced and foreign-made intermediate inputs or consumer goods, (2) other elasticities of substitution in production, and (3) initial domestic oil and gas reserves. Results are summarized in Table 8.

Changing the values of the "Armington" elasticities of substitution between domestic and foreign goods does not dramatically alter the results. One reason for this is that the partial destination-based carbon tax applies equally to domestic and foreign fossil fuels, leaving relative prices of domestic and foreign fossil fuels largely unchanged. This tax puts domestic producers of refined petroleum products at a significant disadvantage relative to their foreign competitors, however, because imported refined petroleum products are not taxed. Higher Armington elasticities imply greater substitution of foreign refined fuels for the domestic counterparts, and greater losses in profits and output in the domestic refined petroleum industry.

Higher values for other elasticities of substitution in production allow for easier substitution on two margins. First, oil and gas can be substituted more easily for coal, which experiences the largest relative price increase.

---

[35] In Goulder (1991a), we examine why carbon taxes tend to be more distortionary than many pre-existing taxes. The carbon tax has a much narrower tax base than that of such taxes as the personal and corporate income taxes. Because the base is narrower, it tends to generate larger gross distortions than those of these other taxes. It should be noted that gross distortions abstract from the efficiency gains associated with environmental (and other externality) effects.

In addition, non-energy inputs can be substituted more easily for energy inputs, which generally rise in price. Both effects contribute to the larger losses to the coal industry when elasticities of substitution are higher.[36] Interestingly, the domestic oil and gas industry fares better under higher production elasticities. Here it is important to note that imported oil and gas is the marginal source of supply, so that a tax-induced reduction in demand for oil and gas primarily affects the residual demand for imports. The importance of higher elasticities to the well-being of the domestic oil and gas industry is its effect on production costs, since there is little demand-side effect to the domestic industry. Under higher production elasticities, the domestic oil and gas industry can more easily contain costs by substituting nonenergy inputs for energy inputs. Thus the magnitude of the loss of profits and output is smaller when the elasticities are higher.

Different assumptions about oil and gas reserves are important mainly for the oil and gas and synthetic fuels industries. For the oil and gas industry, the percentage losses in profits and output tend to be larger in the case where initial reserves are assumed to be larger. Although the losses are greater in percentage terms, the absolute levels of profits and production are higher when higher values are assumed for initial reserves. For example, under the central case assumption of initial oil and gas reserves, the value of domestic oil and gas production in 2020 is $62.8 billion in the baseline and $62.4 billion under the policy change. When initial reserves are assumed to be twice the central value, production in 2020 has a value of $84.8 in the (different) baseline and $84.1 under the policy change. In the synfuels industry, the carbon tax yields somewhat larger losses when higher initial oil and gas reserves are assumed. Baseline levels of synfuels profits and output are also lower under this assumption.

V. CONCLUSIONS

Multilateral initiatives to reduce emissions of carbon dioxide may have many attractions relative to unilateral policies. Many of the "international competitiveness" problems that are so difficult to avoid under unilateral policies simply do not arise under policies that are introduced on a global basis. The advantages of multilateral policies do not eliminate the need for analysis of unilateral programs, however: in view of the difficulties inherent in reaching agreements for coordinated, interna-

---

[36] In the short run, coal profits fall less under the higher production elasticities. This reflects the fact that under this scenario, investment by the coal industry falls by a greater amount. In the short run, the larger drop in investment implies lower adjustment costs, a smaller reduction in retained earnings, and a smaller drop in recorded profits.

TABLE 8.
Sensitivity Analysis
(percentage changes from baseline).

	Coal mining		Oil & Gas extraction		Synthetic fuels	
	1990	2020	1990	2020	1990	2050[1]
1. Central Case						
Domestic Production	−37.14	−40.62	−1.39	−0.51	0.00	−13.18
Profits	−41.09	−38.19	−1.92	−2.51	0.00	−7.06
2. Armington Trade Elasticities						
a. 1.5 × Central Values						
Domestic Production	−36.96	−40.36	−1.38	−0.51	0.00	−13.24
Profits	−41.99	−39.33	−1.92	−2.52	0.00	−7.16
b. 0.5 × Central Values						
Domestic Production	−37.25	−40.86	−1.40	−0.52	0.00	−13.15
Profits	−40.38	−37.20	−1.92	−2.51	0.00	−7.02
3. Production Substitution Elasticities						
a. 1.5 × Central Values						
Domestic Production	−45.12	−49.03	−1.18	−0.39	0.00	−35.93
Profits	−36.60	−44.80	−1.83	−1.84	0.00	−39.15
b. 0.5 × Central Values						
Domestic Production	−32.12	−35.41	−1.67	−0.57	0.00	−11.09
Profits	−44.64	−33.41	−1.98	−2.73	0.00	−9.07
4. Domestic Oil/Gas Reserves						
a. 2.0 × Central Values						
Domestic Production	−37.14	−40.85	−1.39	−0.79	0.00	−13.50
Profits	−41.18	−38.46	−1.91	−3.02	0.00	−7.66
b. 0.5 × Central Values						
Domestic Production	−37.15	−40.37	−1.40	−0.14	0.00	−12.97
Profits	−41.01	−37.84	−1.92	−1.80	0.00	−6.67

tional action, it is worthwhile to investigate closely the potential of unilateral alternatives. This paper has examined various unilateral carbon tax policies, focusing on the distribution of the tax burdens across U.S. industries.

Five main conclusions emerge from this study. First, the burden of a U.S. carbon tax is highly concentrated among a few industries. The coal, oil and gas, petroleum refining, and electricity industries bear the lion's share of the burden from a carbon tax. This reflects the fact that carbon—original and absorbed—is concentrated mainly in these industries.

Second, it makes a great difference to the U.S. coal, oil and gas, and

Petroleum refining		Electric utilities		Gas utilities		Nonenergy manufacturing		Nonenergy services	
1990	2020	1990	2020	1990	2020	1990	2020	1990	2020
−8.91	−5.10	−3.30	−3.99	−2.81	−1.93	−0.31	−0.59	−0.38	−0.58
−6.05	−2.43	−1.30	−1.49	0.55	−0.44	−1.29	−1.48	−1.06	−1.73
−9.45	−5.80	−3.16	−3.84	−2.58	−1.75	−0.30	−0.58	−0.37	−0.57
−7.18	−3.36	−1.37	−1.52	0.59	−0.47	−1.26	−1.49	−1.09	−1.76
−8.44	−4.62	−3.38	−3.99	−2.86	−1.92	−0.32	−0.61	−0.39	−0.59
−5.10	−1.73	−0.97	−1.25	0.66	−0.37	−1.33	−1.49	−1.03	−1.72
−9.94	−4.76	−4.14	−4.37	−3.63	−1.29	−0.41	−0.38	−0.48	−0.46
−2.71	−0.79	−0.36	−0.57	1.72	0.92	−1.28	−1.25	−0.94	−1.42
−8.21	−4.95	−2.76	−3.51	−2.35	−1.95	−0.25	−0.21	−0.32	−0.40
−9.03	−3.09	−2.19	−1.78	−0.56	−1.03	−1.28	−1.11	−1.16	−1.65
−8.90	−5.12	−3.30	−4.00	−2.81	−1.94	−0.30	−0.64	−0.38	−0.60
−6.06	−2.44	−1.31	−1.51	0.53	−0.45	−1.29	−1.54	−1.07	−1.78
−8.91	−5.05	−3.30	−3.95	−2.81	−1.88	−0.32	−0.50	−0.38	−0.54
−6.04	−2.40	−1.31	−1.45	0.55	−0.41	−1.30	−1.41	−1.05	−1.70

[f]For the synfuels industry, percentage changes for 2020 are not meaningful because baseline values are very small in that year. For this reason we report percentage changes for the year 2050.

petroleum refining industries whether the tax is introduced on an origin or destination basis. The reduction in profits to domestic oil and gas producers, for example, is over ten times larger under the origin-based tax, which does not involve tariffs on imported oil, than under the partial or full destination-based taxes, which do.[37]

[37] If the destination-based policy is introduced as a tax on final goods purchased domestically, then the tax will apply to goods of both domestic and foreign origin. Thus imported goods would face a tax, just as they would under the alternative approach involving import tariffs.

Third, for most U.S. industries it makes relatively little difference whether one introduces a partial or a full destination-based carbon tax. For the petroleum refining industry, however, the breadth of the application of the destination principle makes a dramatic difference: To avoid substantial costs to petroleum refiners, the carbon tax would have to apply not only to imported fossil fuels but to imported refined products as well. Extending the destination principle even further—widening the base of the tax to cover other carbon-based products—helps preserve international competitiveness for a broader range of industries, but makes administration of the tax more problematic. It is difficult to gauge where the appropriate balance between safeguarding competitiveness and limiting administrative costs is best struck. An examination of the distribution of carbon content across produced goods suggests, however, that the application of the destination principle to a relatively small number of carbon-intensive products would avert the most significant potential impacts on international competitiveness while avoiding the substantial administrative costs that the full destination-based carbon tax would entail.

Fourth, destination-based U.S. carbon taxes are much more effective than origin-based taxes in reducing U.S. demands for carbon-based goods and the associated emissions. Under an origin-based tax, about 57% of the reduction in U.S.-source emissions is offset by increased net imports of emissions through substitution toward more carbon-intensive products. Under the destination-based alternatives, there is little substitution of this kind because in this case carbon-intensive imports gain no cost advantage relative to the domestically produced counterparts. A partial destination-based carbon tax achieves over 90 percent of the reduction in U.S. consumption of emissions that would occur under a full destination-based tax. The move from a partial to a full destination-based tax would have only a modest effect on emissions, yet the increase in administrative costs of such a move could be quite large. This calls in question the advisability of attempting to achieve a fully destination-based carbon tax.

Finally, using carbon tax revenues to finance cuts in other distortionary taxes reduces, but does not eliminate, the adverse consequences of the carbon tax policy for industry profits and investment. When the revenues are used this way, fossil fuel producers and producers of fossil-fuel-intensive products lose less than they would if revenues were returned in lump-sum fashion, but the losses do not vanish. Aggregate efficiency results suggest that a carbon tax must inevitably generate losses for at least some industries.

Although this analysis helps clarify the attractions and drawbacks of alternative types of carbon taxes, it leaves unanswered the question whether a carbon tax is preferable to other policies to achieve reductions in carbon dioxide emissions. The analysis also leaves open the question of what size (if any) carbon tax would be best. Answering this latter question requires attention to the value of the environmental benefits stemming from reduced carbon dioxide emissions. The magnitudes of these benefits are likely to remain highly uncertain for a long time. Still, policy choices—which may include the decision to avoid introducing a carbon tax—will have to be made in the short term, before the uncertainties are resolved. An analytical framework that could help guide today's choices is that of (sequential) decision making under uncertainty. There is considerable room for research that employs this framework to analyze the carbon tax and other environmental policy options in an uncertain world.

APPENDIX A: DETERMINING CARBON CONTENT AND
DESIGNING A DESTINATION-BASED CARBON TAX

1. Calculating the Carbon Content of Fossil-Fuel-Based Products

Let n represent the number of industries, including the fossil-fuel-producing industries. Let b_i (i = 1, . . . ,n) denote the content of original carbon in the output of industry i. This is the amount of carbon that is found naturally in fossil fuels. Only fossil fuels have original carbon; for industries other than fossil fuels, b_i is zero. Let a_{ij} represent the required input of good i per unit of output produced by industry j.[38] Then e_j, the total embodied carbon content of product j, can be expressed as

$$e_j = b_j + \sum_{i=1}^{n} b_i a_{ij} + \sum_{k=1}^{n} \sum_{i=1}^{n} b_k a_{ki} a_{ij}$$

$$+ \sum_{m=1}^{n} \sum_{k=1}^{n} \sum_{i=1}^{n} b_m a_{mk} a_{ki} a_{ij} + \ldots \qquad (1)$$

The first term on the right-hand side is the original carbon content. The other terms indicate *absorbed* carbon: the second term is the carbon content of the fuels used as inputs in the production of good j, the third is the carbon content of fuels used as inputs to the inputs to product j, etc.[39]

---

[38] Each element a_{ij} includes both domestic and foreign-made inputs of type i per unit of output j.

[39] Equation (1) indicates that the total carbon associated with a unit of processed or extracted fuel will generally exceed the fuel's original carbon content.

In matrix form, equation (1) can be written as:

$$e = b + bA + bA^2 + bA^3 + \ldots \tag{2}$$

where e and b are n-length row vectors, and A is an n by n matrix. This infinite series can be expressed as:

$$e = b[I-A]^{-1} \tag{3}$$

We employ equation (3) to calculate the total embodied (original plus absorbed) carbon content of each produced good.

2. Calculating Import Levies and Export Subsidies for a Destination-Based Carbon Tax Policy.

The purpose of import levies and export subsidies under a destination-based carbon tax is to eliminate the cost disadvantage which would otherwise occur as a result of a carbon tax. First consider the firms' costs in the absence of a carbon tax. Assuming a competitive environment in which price equals cost, the relationship between input prices, factor costs, and output prices can be expressed as:

$$p_j(1-t_{oj}) = \sum_{i=1}^{n} p_i(1+t_{ij})a_{ij} + v_j \tag{4}$$

where p_j is the price of product j (gross of output taxes), t_{oj} is the output tax on product j, t_{ij} is the tax on intermediate use of good i by industry j, and v_j is the unit factor (capital and labor) cost of good j.[40] This formulation assumes constant-returns-to-scale production: costs are independent of the scale of output.

In matrix form we can express this relationship as:

$$pT_1 = p\tilde{A} + v \tag{5}$$

where p is a 1 by n vector of prices, T_1 is an n by n diagonal matrix consisting of diagonal elements $1-t_{oj}$ ($j = 1, \ldots, n$), $\tilde{A}$ is an n by n matrix consisting of elements $(1+t_{ij})a_{ij}$, and v is a 1 by n vector of unit factor costs. The solution to the system represented by (5) is:

$$p = v[T_1-\tilde{A}]^{-1} \tag{6}$$

---

[40] Equation (4) implicitly assumes that there are no tariffs on imported inputs. The extension to incorporate tariffs is straightforward and involves distinguishing the domestic and foreign inputs required per unit of production.

Now consider the cost increase which would result from an origin-based carbon tax. Let t_{cj} represent the carbon tax levied on industry j. In contrast with the *ad valorem* output tax t_{oj}, the carbon tax is a per-unit tax. The tax is proportional to original carbon content, b_j. Thus t_{cj} is nonzero only for the fossil-fuel-producing industries. With the carbon tax, the relationship between price and cost becomes:

$$p_j(1-t_{oj}) - t_{cj} = \sum_{i=1}^{n} p_i(1+t_{ij})a_{ij} + v_j \tag{7}$$

In matrix form this is:

$$pT_1 - t_c = p\tilde{A} + v \tag{8}$$

The solution to this system is:

$$p = (v+t_c)(T_1-\tilde{A})^{-1} \tag{9}$$

The cost effect of the carbon tax is given by the difference between the prices in equations (6) and (9).[41] The difference is $t_c(T_1-\tilde{A})^{-1}$. This can be rewritten as:

$$t_cT_1^{-1} + t_c(T_1^{-1}\tilde{A})T_1^{-1} + t_c(T_1^{-1}\tilde{A})^2T_1^{-1} + \dots \tag{10}$$

The first term in equation (10) is nonzero only for the fossil-fuel-producing industries; it is the cost increase associated with the direct application of the carbon tax to the output of that industry. The second term (generally nonzero in all industries) represents the cost increase stemming from higher-priced fossil fuel inputs used by the industry. The remaining terms represent the effect from higher-priced fossil fuels used indirectly by the industry, that is, from higher prices of other inputs to the industry as a result of the carbon tax having raised the costs of these inputs.

To neutralize the effect of a carbon tax on the costs of exported goods, it is necessary to introduce a per-unit subsidy to each exported product j equal to $\sum_{i=1}^{n} t_{ci}X_{ij}$, where $X \equiv (T_1-\tilde{A})^{-1}$ from (9). This restores the after-tax cost of the exported good to its original value given in (6).[42] Similarly, an

[41] This analysis assumes that the carbon tax does not alter the technical coefficients that make up the matrix **A**. To the extent that firms can change input intensities to reduce the use of the taxed inputs, the cost effect will be smaller than that given here.

[42] The subsidy allows domestic producers to continue to devote products to the export market. The subsidy has no direct impact on domestic producers' decisions to sell on the export market as opposed to the domestic market. Although producers enjoy the subsidy

import levy equal $\Sigma_{i=1}^n t_{ci}X_{ij}$ for imported good j would cause imported fossil-based products to increase in price by the same amount as domestically-produced goods of the same type.[43]

In the special case where there are no prior output taxes t_j or intermediate good taxes t_{ij}, **X** reduces to $[\mathbf{I} - \mathbf{A}]^{-1}$, indicating that the cost increase of a carbon tax in a given industry is proportional to the quantity of original and absorbed carbon embodied in a unit of output.

APPENDIX B: FUNCTIONAL FORMS AND PARAMETERS USED IN THE MODEL[44]

1. *Industry Production Functions and Elasticities*

a. Production Structure (see text for definitions of variables):
   —industries other than oil and gas industry:

$$X = f[g(L,K), h(E,M)] - \phi(I/K) \cdot I$$

—oil and gas industry:

$$X = \gamma(Z) \cdot f[g(L,K),h(E,M)] - \phi(I/K) \cdot I$$

—all industries:

$$E = E(\bar{x}_2, \bar{x}_3+\bar{x}_4, \bar{x}_5, \ldots , \bar{x}_7)$$
$$M = M(\bar{x}_1, \bar{x}_8, \ldots , \bar{x}_{13})$$

where $\bar{x}_i$ is a composite of domestically produced and foreign made input i. Industry indices correspond to those of the first table under c.

b. Functional Forms:
   —f, g, h, E, M, and $\bar{x}$ functions (all industries): CES
   —ϕ adjustment cost function (all industries):

only for exported goods, they cannot enjoy higher profits from exports unless they raise export prices. The latter would reduce foreign demands for the exported goods. At unchanged export prices, the subsidy simply permits exporters to maintain their profit margins.

[43] Note that if the technology employed in producing imports differed from that used in producing the corresponding domestic goods, then this import levy will not generally imply the same tax rate per unit of carbon content as that applied to domestic goods through the carbon tax.

[44] See Cruz and Goulder (1991) for documentation of data and parameter sources.

$$\phi(I/K) = \left[\begin{array}{l} \dfrac{1}{2} \cdot \beta \cdot (I/K - \delta)^2 / (I/K) \, , \, I/K > \delta \\ \\ 0 \qquad\qquad\qquad\qquad , \, I/K \le \delta \end{array} \right.$$

δ represents the rate of economic depreciation.

—γ stock effect function (oil and gas industry):

$$\gamma(Z_t) = \gamma_0 - (Z_t/\bar{Z})^\epsilon$$

$$Z_t = Z_0 + \sum_{s=1}^{t-1} X_s$$

Z_t is cumulative extraction (output) of oil/gas up to the beginning of period t and $\bar{Z}$ is total discovered reserves.

c. Parameter Values:

—elasticities of substitution in production:

				Substitution Margin:	
				E	*M*
Producing Industry	*g-h*	*L-K*	*E-M*	*components*	*components*
1. Agriculture and Non-coal Mining	0.7	0.68	0.7	1.45	0.6
2. Coal Mining	0.7	0.80	0.7	1.08	0.6
3. Oil and Gas Extraction	0.7	0.82	0.7	1.04	0.6
4. Synthetic Fuels	0.7	0.82	0.7	1.04	0.6
5. Petroleum Refining	0.7	0.74	0.7	1.04	0.6
6. Electric Utilities	0.7	0.81	0.7	0.97	0.6
7. Gas Utilities	0.7	0.96	0.7	1.04	0.6
8. Construction	0.7	0.95	0.7	1.04	0.6
9. Metals and Machinery	0.7	0.91	0.7	1.21	0.6
10. Motor Vehicles	0.7	0.80	0.7	1.04	0.6
11. Miscellaneous Manufacturing	0.7	0.94	0.7	1.08	0.6
12. Services (except electric utilities, gas utilities, and housing)	0.7	0.98	0.7	1.07	0.6
13. Housing Services	0.7	0.80	0.7	1.81	0.6

—elasticities of substitution between domestic and foreign inputs (parameter of $\bar{x}$ functions)

Input Type	elasticity
1. Agriculture and Non-coal Mining	2.31
2. Coal Mining	1.14
3. Oil and Gas Extraction	(infinite)
4. Synthetic Fuels	(not traded)
5. Petroleum Refining	2.21
6. Electric Utilities	1.0
7. Gas Utilities	1.0
8. Construction	1.0
9. Metals and Machinery	2.74
10. Motor Vehicles	1.14
11. Miscellaneous Manufacturing	2.74
12. Services (except electric utilities, gas utilities, and housing)	1.0
13. Housing Services	(not traded)

—stock effect function parameters:

parameter:	Z_0	$\bar{Z}$	γ_0	ϵ
value:	0	450	1	2

Note: This function is parameterized so that γ approaches 0 as Z approaches $\bar{Z}$. The value of $\bar{Z}$ is 450 billion barrels (about 100 times the 1990 production of oil and gas, where gas is measured in barrel-equivalents). $\bar{Z}$ is based on estimates from Masters et al. (1987). Investment in new oil and gas capital ceases to be profitable before reserves are depleted: the value of ϵ implies that, in the baseline scenario, oil and gas investment becomes zero in the year 2031.

2. Household Utility Function

a. Utility Function:

$$U_t = \sum_{s=t}^{\infty} (1+\omega)^{t-s} \frac{\sigma}{\sigma-1} C_s^{\frac{\sigma-1}{\sigma}}$$

where ω is the subjective rate of time preference, σ is the intertemporal elasticity of substitution in consumption, and C is CES, a composite of consumption of goods and services G and leisure L:

$$C_s = \left[G_s^{\frac{v-1}{v}} + \eta^{\frac{1}{v}} L_s^{\frac{v-1}{v}} \right]^{\frac{v}{v-1}}$$

b. Parameter Values:

parameter:	ω	σ	v	η
value:	0.007	0.5	0.69	0.84

REFERENCES

Barro, Robert (1979). "On the Determination of the Public Debt." *Journal of Political Economy* 87, 940–971.

Cruz, Miguel, and Lawrence H. Goulder (1991). "An Intertemporal General Equilibrium Model for Analyzing U.S. Environmental and Energy Policies: Data Documentation." Working paper, Stanford University, June.

Goulder, Lawrence H. (1990). "Using Carbon Charges to Combat Global Climate Change." Stanford University Center for Economic Policy Research Discussion Paper No. 226, December.

_____ (1991b). "Second-Best Taxation and Non-Renewable Resource Supply: An Integrative Approach." Working paper, Stanford University, March.

_____ (1991a). "Effects of Carbon Taxes in an Economy with Prior Tax Distortions: An Intertemporal General Equilibrium Analysis for the U.S." Working paper, Stanford University, June.

Goulder, Lawrence H., and Lawrence H. Summers (1989). "Tax Policy, Asset Prices, and Growth: A General Equilibrium Analysis." *Journal of Public Economics* 38, 265–296.

Jorgenson, Dale W., and Peter J. Wilcoxen (1990). "Reducing U.S. Carbon Dioxide Emissions: The Cost of Different Goals." Working paper, Harvard University, November.

Lave, Lester (1991). "Formulating Greenhouse Policies in a Sea of Uncertainty" *The Energy Journal* 12(1), 9–21, January.

Manne, Alan S., and Richard G. Richels (1990a). "CO$_2$ Emission Limits: An Economic Analysis for the USA." *The Energy Journal* 11 (2), 51–85.

_____(1990b). "Global CO$_2$ Emission Reductions—The Impacts of Rising Energy Costs." Working paper, Stanford University, February.

_____ (1992). *Buying Greenhouse Insurance: The Economic Costs of CO$_2$ Emissions Limits*. Cambridge, Mass.: The MIT Press, forthcoming.

Masters, Charles D., et al. (1987). "World Resources of Crude Oil, Natural Gas, Natural Bitumen, and Shale Oil." In *Proceedings of the 12th World Petroleum Congress* 5, 3–27.

Mussa, Michael (1978). "Dynamic Adjustment in a Heckscher-Ohlin-Samuelson Model." *Journal of Political Economy* 86 (5), 775–791.

Nordhaus, William (1990). "To Slow or Not to Slow: The Economics of the Greenhouse Effect." Paper prepared for the 1990 annual meeting of the American Association for the Advancement of Science.

———— (1991). "The Cost of Slowing Climate Change: A Survey." *The Energy Journal* 12 (1), January.

OECD/IEA (1990). *Energy Balances of OECD Countries: 1987–1988.* Paris: OECD.

———— (1991). *Oil and Gas Information, 1988–1990.* Paris: OECD.

Peck, Stephen C., and Thomas J. Teisberg (1991). "CETA: A Model for Carbon Emissions Trajectory Assessment." Working paper, Electric Power Research Institute, February.

Poterba, James M. (1991). "Tax Policy to Combat Global Warming: On Designing a Carbon Tax." National Bureau of Economic Research Working Paper No. 3649, March.

Sandmo, Agnar (1975). "Optimal Taxation in the Presence of Externalities." *Swedish Journal of Economics* 77, 86–98.

Shiells, Clinton R., Robert M. Stern, and Alan V. Deardorff (1986). "Estimates of the Elasticities of Substitution between Imports and Home Goods for the United States." *Weltwirtschaftliches Archiv* 122: 497–519.

U.S. Department of Commerce (1984). *Survey of Current Business,* May.

———— (1991). *Survey of Current Business,* February.

U.S. Department of Energy, Energy Information Administration (1989). *Annual Energy Outlook 1989, Long Term Projections.*

U.S. Environmental Protection Agency (1989). *Policy Options for Stabilizing Global Climate.* Draft Report to the Congress, Daniel Lashof and Dennis Tirpak, eds., February.

Weyant, John (1991). "Global Climate Change: Energy Sector Impacts of Greenhouse Gas Emission Control Strategies," Working paper, Energy Modeling Forum, Stanford University, March.

World Resources Institute (1990). *World Resources: 1990–91.* New York: Oxford University Press.

TAXATION AND INEQUALITY: A TIME-EXPOSURE PERSPECTIVE

Joel Slemrod
The University of Michigan and NBER

I. INTRODUCTION

There is a wide consensus among economists that the distribution of income in the United States recently has become more unequal. Most observers believe that this trend was well under way by 1980; many trace its origin to as early as 1970. There is less consensus about the causes of the growth in inequality. Among the competing hypotheses are a shift in demand toward high-skilled labor and away from unskilled labor, an increase in the relative supply of low-skilled workers, and a shift in output toward sectors where individuals' productivities are more variable and more easily identified.

There is virtually no consensus about the role of the tax system in the growth in inequality, and swirling controversy about the appropriate tax policy response to this trend. For example, Gramlich, Kasten, and

Prepared for the National Bureau of Economic Research Conference on Tax Policy and the Economy, to be held November 19 in Washington, D.C. I am grateful to Marianne Page and Alec Rodney for exemplary research assistance, and to Shlomo Yitzhaki for providing key computer programs used in the analysis. Helpful comments on an earlier draft were provided by Don Fullerton, Roger Gordon, Ned Gramlich, Rick Kasten, Donald Kiefer, Jim Poterba, Frank Sammartino, Bob Williams, and Shlomo Yitzhaki.

Sammartino (1991) have claimed that, in the 1980s, the tax system became slightly less effective in reducing the inequality in pre-tax incomes. Lindsey (1990) has argued that the precipitous drop at the start of the 1980s in the marginal tax rate imposed on higher income individuals was a principal cause of the increased apparent inequality of pre-tax incomes, because it has encouraged these individuals to work more, report more income, realize more capital gains, and convert nontaxed compensation to taxable compensation. Finally, many of the tax policy changes currently being advocated, in particular the child credit financed by higher tax rates on higher-income taxpayers, are justified in part as an attempt to offset the increase in income inequality.

Nearly all of the conclusions about the trend in inequality and the role of the tax system have been based on cross-sectional snapshots of annual income. Yet it is well known that conclusions based on snapshots can give a misleading picture of the inequality of a more permanent notion of income, due to the mobility of individuals across annual income classes. Specifically, transitory income will give the appearance of greater inequality in a one-year snapshot than over a longer period. If the relative importance of transitory income has changed over time, then the trends in the inequality of annual income may misstate the trends in a more permanent notion of income. Furthermore, most of the conclusions about inequality have been based on either labor earnings or the Current Population Survey (CPS) definition of money income, which excludes capital gains, poorly measures other capital income, and is subject to coded maximum values.

In this paper I make use of tax return data that has extensive information on property income, and in particular two longitudinal tax return data bases that follow an unchanging sample of taxpayers from 1979 to 1986, and a distinct set of taxpayers from 1967 to 1973, in order to reassess some of the conclusions about taxation and inequality. The paper is arranged as follows. Section II provides a brief review of what is known, based on snapshots, of inequality over the past two decades. Section III utilizes tax return data to investigate some of these same issues, with an emphasis on decomposing the trends by source of income. In Section IV I bring to bear the 1979–1986 longitudinal data file of tax returns, and reassess some of the earlier results; Section V compares these results to the 1967–1973 panel. Section VI summarizes the findings and restates the caveats to be applied to these findings.

II. INEQUALITY AND TAXES:
A BRIEF REVIEW OF THE LITERATURE

A. *Trends in Inequality*

There is a broad consensus that income inequality has been increasing in the last two decades. There is evidence of increased dispersion since the mid-1970s in both the lower and upper tails of the distribution for families and for individuals, and in the distribution of labor income for workers. At least since 1979, inequality has grown both between less and more educated workers and also among apparently similar workers. As Karoly (1991) has documented, this conclusion is robust to a great variety of disaggregations, including by families with children and race-ethnicity. The increase in inequality among workers cannot simply be explained by shifts in the gender, education or experience composition of the work force, and is evident even when the sample is restricted to full-time workers.

Several alternative explanations have been offered to the increased inequality. Most attention has been paid to labor market factors, as labor market income accounts for about 70 percent of family income. Among the supply explanations offered are shifts in the size of worker-age cohorts and the educational distribution of these cohorts. Among the demand explanations offered are shifts in the composition of final output, in the occupational mix within industries, in skill requirements, and in the density of unionization. The strength of the evidence supporting these not mutually exclusive explanations is assessed in Levy and Murnane (1991).

B. *Taxes as an Offset to Growing Inequality*

Although the CPS measure of income is before taxation, it is clear that after-tax income is a superior measure of well-being. With that in mind, it is interesting to know to what extent the tax system has offset, or exacerbated, the increased inequality in pre-tax income. Using CPS data supplemented by data from tax returns, Gramlich, Kasten, and Sammartino (1991) conclude that during the 1980s tax and transfer policy changes became less effective in reducing pre-tax income inequality. As a result, after-tax income inequality increased by even more than pre-tax income inequality. Of a 16.5 percent increase in the Gini coefficient of post-tax, post-transfer income between 1980 and 1990, they attribute 40 percent to the decline in the redistributive effectiveness of the federal tax and transfer system, with the 40 percent about equally divided between taxes and transfers. Some of the change in the distribution of transfers and taxes was, however, the result of economic and demographic changes rather than explicit changes in policy. When they hold the distribution of pre-tax, pre-transfer income at its 1990 level but adjust transfers and taxes to reflect 1980 law, only 16 percent of the increase in the inequality of post-tax, post-transfer income was due to policy changes. Most of these policy changes involved a decrease in the progressivity of federal taxes, due to the increased importance of the regressive social security taxes; also significant was a fall in the share of transfers going to low-income people.

C. Taxes as an Inducement to Growing Inequality

The previous calculation ignores the possibility that the tax system induces changes in pre-tax income. Lindsey (1990) has argued that in the early 1980s the sharply reduced marginal tax rates at the top (which fell in 1981 from 70 percent to 50 percent, in 1987 to 39 percent, and in 1988 to 28 percent) induced high-income taxpayers to work more hours, report a higher share of their income to the Internal Revenue Service, realize more capital gains, take more compensation in taxable form, and generally substitute taxable income for either nontaxed income or leisure.

This argument implies that much of the apparent increase in the dispersion of income in the 1980s is illusory. The high incomes were there, prior to 1981, but they were in forms that would either not appear in the standard data sets on income, not be realized income sources, or were potential income consumed in the form of leisure. This important and controversial claim is not addressed directly in the analysis that follows, although the data sources described next can help to assess its validity.

D. Public Finance Implications of Inequality

An accurate picture of the distribution of income and its sources is critical for at least two important questions in public finance: How is the burden of any given tax system shared by individuals, and how should the tax burden be shared across income classes?

There are two steps to understanding how the burden of taxation is borne. In the first step, known to economists as the question of tax incidence, knowledge of the price sensitivity of supply and demand is used to predict the extent to which a tax will be borne by the statutory bearer of the burden—the "check writer"—and the extent to which the burden will be shifted to others through changes in prices. In the second step the conclusions about how prices will be affected is translated into how families' well being is changed. This step requires information about the distribution of wealth, potential labor income, and tastes. For example, once a judgment is made about how a cigarette tax will change the price of cigarettes and the value of tobacco land, one needs to know the distribution of demand for cigarettes, unskilled labor, and ownership of tobacco land.

The distribution of income-earning ability is also a critical input into the modern theory of optimal tax progressivity, which poses the problem as a tradeoff between the social benefit of a more equal distribution of well-being and the disincentive cost of the tax and transfer system needed to effect a more equal distribution. In the standard models of this literature, described in Slemrod (1983), a more unequal distribution of inherent abilities—or the return to these abilities—increases the optimal degree of progressivity because it increases the social value of the redistribution accomplished for any given degree of tax progressivity. Another strand of the literature, exemplified by Varian (1980), stresses the social insurance function of progressive taxation. In this framework, an increase in exogenous variability of income would also increase the optimal degree of progressivity, because it increases the insurance value of the progressivity.

III. SNAPSHOT DISTRIBUTIONS

A. Why Snapshots May Mislead

Many of the conclusions about the distribution of these factors are based on snapshots of the distribution taken at a point of time. It is critical to realize, however, that snapshots of distributions can give a highly misleading picture of the distribution of a more permanent notion of income or well-being. As an illustration, consider an economy of individuals who are identical except for their age, where each individual follows the same life-cycle pattern of increasing labor income over the working years, followed by a period of retirement with no labor income. A snapshot of the distribution of labor income would conclude that to the extent a tax lowers after-tax wage income, it will have a highly skewed burden distribution, severely affecting some individuals (the working young) and leaving others unscathed (the retired elderly). But, of course, from a lifetime perspective (except for transitional effects) everyone is equally affected, as everyone will at some time be at the high labor income age and also the retirement age. In addition to life-cycle effects, a measure of inequality based on a snapshot will capture intercohort effects due to real income growth over time.

This paper focuses on a separate reason why a snapshot may give a misleading picture of the distribution of income sources—transitory income. An example will best convey the problem. Imagine an economy where individuals have but two sources of income. One source, which I will call labor income, is equally distributed across individuals and stable over time. The other source, which I will call capital gains, also is equally distributed but is also highly unstable over time; every so often an exogenous process conveys capital gains income to some individuals. A snapshot of any year's distribution of income sources will reveal two "facts": (1) that the distribution of total income is more unequal than that of labor income alone and (2) that capital gains are a more important source of income for high-income individuals. These facts will appear even though, over the long run, capital gains income is distributed no differently than labor income and all individuals have equal income.

There is one more twist to this story. In the above illustration it was assumed that the time pattern of capital gains income was exogenously determined. In reality the timing of the realization of income for tax purposes may be subject to a great deal of control by the individual. In particular, because of the graduated nature of the income tax system, there is an incentive for individuals to use their discretion over the timing of some income to smooth taxable income over time. Not only capital gains realizations, but to some extent the taxable income from business, can be subject to this kind of "self-averaging." Other transitory components of income, such as those due to unemployment or income windfalls, are essentially exogenous to the taxpayer.

The goal of this research program is to separate out the effect of transitory income on measured inequality, so as to get a better measure of the nature of, and trends in, a more permanent notion of inequality.

B. Measuring Inequality Using Tax Return Data

Most analysis of trends in U.S. inequality have relied on the data in the Current Population Surveys (CPS), conducted by the Census Bureau in March of most years. The analysis that follows is based on the data from the Internal Revenue Service (IRS) Statistics of Income Division's public-use files of tax return information. This shift in data sources has its advantages and disadvantages, which I detail below.

An important advantage of the CPS is that it is designed to be a sample of the entire population and is therefore not restricted, for example, to tax filers. It also collects a wide variety of demographic information, including details about family structure and earnings disaggregated by family member. One disadvantage of the CPS is its poor coverage of capital income. Realized capital gains are not included at all, and other components of realized capital income are apparently severely underreported. In addition, all components of income, as well as total family income, are top-coded, so that there is no information on the upper tail of the distribution of income or its components. Clearly both of these problems are especially important in the analysis of the high-income population.

The strengths and weaknesses of the tax model data mirror those of the CPS. It covers only households that file tax returns, so it systematically excludes households whose low income makes them exempt from filing and who do not file a return in order to receive a refundable credit. It also excludes those who illegally fail to file a return. There is very little demographic information. On the plus side, the tax model data has very rich information on taxable sources of capital income, and is not top-coded.

C. Trends in Snapshot Inequality

Table 1 presents some summary information about the changes in the distribution of after-tax income, and its components, over the last two decades. The income concept used here, called expanded income, begins with adjusted gross income and then adds to it excluded long-term capital gains, excluded dividends and all adjustments. When an after-tax concept is used, tax liability net of credits is subtracted from expanded income. These changes are designed to make the income concept more comparable across years.

Expanded income is by no means an ideal measure of annual income. Among the problems are the failure to correct capital income for inflation, the exclusion of the rental value of owner-occupied homes and other consumer durables, the failure to subtract real interest payments, and the inclusion of capital gains on a realization, rather than an accrual, basis. Nevertheless, because many studies of tax return data use income concepts with these characteristics, it is important to understand the nature of inequality measures that are based on this type of information.

In Table 1 I make use of the Gini coefficient as a measure of inequality.[1] The numbers in the first row document a striking increase in the inequality of after-tax expanded income between 1972 and 1988; the Gini coefficient rises from 0.445 to 0.544 over this period. For pre-tax income the increase is from .468 in 1972 to .496 in 1980 and .567 in 1988. This is broadly consistent with the Gramlich, Kasten, and Sammartino (1991) result that the Gini of pre-tax, pre-transfer income rose from 0.473 in

---

[1] I am grateful to Shlomo Yitzhaki for providing the computer programs for calculating the Gini coefficient and decomposition discussed here. The figures of Table 1 are based on random subsamples of approximately 15,000 per year of the Individual Tax Model Files, a stratified random sample of about 100,000 tax returns made publicly available by the Statistics of Income Division of the Internal Revenue Service.

TABLE 1.

Gini Coefficients and Decomposition of After-Tax Expanded Income and its Components and Pre-Tax Expanded Income, 1972–1988.

	1972			1976		
	Gini	Share	Rho	Gini	Share	Rho
Expanded income after tax	0.445			0.458		
Wages and salaries	0.489	0.927	0.856	0.515	0.948	0.856
Capital gains	1.052	0.055	0.760	1.066	0.042	0.733
Interest	0.884	0.041	0.438	0.883	0.051	0.457
Dividends	0.981	0.026	0.712	0.982	0.024	0.734
Schedule C	1.188	0.053	0.562	1.286	0.047	0.542
Schedule E	1.713	0.029	0.509	2.144	0.024	0.422
Schedule F	2.465	0.006	0.320	6.664	0.003	0.326
Pension	0.976	0.016	0.279	0.962	0.030	0.303
Other income	+2.716	−0.007	+0.006	−1.937	−0.014	0.029
Tax	+0.654	−0.146	+0.957	+0.682	−0.155	+0.960
Expanded income before tax	0.468			0.485		

1980 to 0.513 in 1985 and an estimated 0.523 in 1990. Table 1 also presents the Gini coefficient and shares of each of several components of after-tax income.[2] It also lists, under the columns headed "rho," the Gini correlation between the component and after-tax income.[3] As discussed in Lerman and Yitzhaki (1985), the Gini coefficient of income can be decomposed so that it is equal to the sum, over all components, of the product of the component's own Gini, its share in income, and the Gini correlation.

Because wages and salaries represent about 90 percent of after-tax income (and about 80 percent of pre-tax income), it is reasonable to look there for the origin of the change in inequality, and this strategy is rewarded. The second row of Table 1 reveals that between 1972 and 1988 the Gini coefficient of wages and salaries increased from 0.489 to 0.578. Clearly a large part of the trend in overall inequality is associated with the increased inequality of wages and salaries.

[2] The astute reader will notice the prevalence of Gini coefficients for income components that are in excess of one. This is due to the presence of negative values for these components, which means that the Lorenz curve lies partly below the x-axis.

[3] The Gini correlation of component k is the ratio of the covariance of k with the observation's rank in the income distribution and the covariance of k with the rank in the distribution of k. It ranges between −1 and +1, taking on a value of +1 if the ranking by income and the ranking by k are identical.

1980			1984			1988		
Gini	Share	Rho	Gini	Share	Rho	Gini	Share	Rho
0.467			0.502			0.544		
0.526	0.937	0.854	0.554	0.909	0.853	0.578	0.882	0.867
1.088	0.053	0.781	1.061	0.070	0.780	1.086	0.062	0.781
0.886	0.074	0.489	0.869	0.091	0.457	0.888	0.069	0.487
0.975	0.030	0.773	0.963	0.026	0.686	0.967	0.029	0.666
1.408	0.040	0.490	1.446	0.039	0.433	1.271	0.046	0.494
4.581	0.053	0.270	653.00	0.000	0.210	3.582	0.020	0.497
−8.925	−0.002	0.315	−1.844	−0.007	0.167	−37.74	0.000	0.182
0.955	0.034	0.255	0.945	0.041	0.348	0.932	0.067	0.490
289.38	0.000	0.385	−3.805	−0.012	0.226	−3.578	−0.011	0.520
+0.682	−0.179	+0.957	+0.687	−0.159	+0.956	+0.731	−0.164	+0.962
0.496			0.524			0.567		

Source: Random subsamples (of approximately 15,000 per year) of Individual Income Tax Model files.
Note: Gini coefficients of sources of income with a share close to zero are unreliable indicators of the skewness of the distribution.

For all the years, subtracting tax liability reduces the dispersion of income as measured by the Gini, although the change is fairly small. In 1972 the reduction is 0.023. It peaks in 1980 at 0.029, when the ratio of tax liability to after-tax expanded income also reaches its peak of 0.179. It declines in 1984 back to 0.022 and then turns slightly up in 1988 to 0.023. Thus the federal income tax liability has done little, if anything, to offset the increasing dispersion of pre-tax incomes; in the 1980s it has slightly exacerbated the trend toward increased inequality of after-tax incomes, holding pre-tax incomes unchanged.

Comparing the Gini coefficient of pre-tax and post-tax incomes answers the question of what a total elimination of federal income taxes would do to inequality. Another meaningful question is how a marginal proportional change in taxes would affect overall income inequality. Lerman and Yitzhaki (1985) show that a 1 percent change in component k changes the overall Gini by $s_k(p_k G_k − G)/100$, where s_k, p_k and G_k are the share, Gini correlation, and own Gini of component k, respectively, and G is the overall Gini. Performing this calculation reveals that a proportional 10 percent increase in taxes would have reduced the overall Gini in 1972 by 0.00264, or 0.59 percent of its actual value. By 1988, the same experiment would have reduced the overall Gini by 0.00262, or 0.48 percent of its actual value.[4]

IV. TIME-EXPOSURE INCOME

D. *The Importance of Transitory Income*

The presence of transitory income, and the mobility of taxpayers across income classes, means that inequality of income in any given snapshot can exceed that of a more permanent notion of income, and that conclusions on the contribution of any source of income to inequality based on snapshots can be misleading. In this section I present some evidence on the importance of these issues for the period 1979 to 1986.

The source of this information is a panel of individual tax returns. Beginning in 1979, the IRS Statistics of Income Division has been collecting information from the tax returns of a randomly selected group of taxpayers. This panel, known as the Continuous Work History File, was developed for internal use, but the IRS has made this longitudinal data set available to academic researchers through a special arrangement with the Office of Tax Policy Research at the University of Michigan, in conjunction with the Ernst & Young Tax Research Database. The panel now spans 1979 to 1986, with 1987 and 1988 expected soon. The panel is a nonstratified random sample chosen on the basis of the last four digits of the primary taxpayer's social security number (SSN). Of those numbers chosen, anyone filing a return is included in the sample. The first three years of the panel each contain in excess of 45,000 returns, though the last three years of the panel show a substantial drop in the number of observations (approximately 9,000 in 1982, 1984, and 1986, 19,000 in 1983 and 1985) due to budgetary limitations at the IRS.[5] Pooling all observations in the panel gives a sample size of 177,177. Due largely to the small number of observations in 1982, 1984, and 1986, the number of individu-

---

[4] Note that this procedure implies that a 100 percent reduction in taxes (i.e., complete elimination) would increase the Gini in 1988 by 0.0262, whereas the actual difference between the pre-tax and after-tax Gini is only 0.023. The discrepancy is due to the fact that the calculation in the text is precise only at the margin. Any nonincremental change in taxes would require a reranking of taxpayers by after-tax income, which would increase the Gini. For this reason the marginal calculation applied to the complete elimination of taxes overstates the actual difference between pre- and after-tax Gini coefficients.

[5] The sample is drawn on the basis of the last four digits of the social security number of the primary (first listed on the tax return) taxpayer. In 1979 through 1981 the sample includes all returns filed in a calendar year with any of five four-digit endings. In 1982 only those returns with one of the five endings were drawn; in 1983 returns with two of the endings were chosen. The alternating one-ending, two-ending cycle was continued through 1986.

als present in all eight years of the panel is limited to 5,780 taxpayers. The information contained in each observation is a subset of the information on the standard forms filed by the taxpayer, and varies slightly from year to year.

Attrition from the panel may occur for a number of reasons unrelated to deliberate change in the sample size, including death, a change in marital status, income below the minimum that would trigger filing, or simply the choice of which spouse (between two married, joint filers) is listed first on the tax form (and thus becomes the "primary" taxpayer whose SSN is the basis of selection). A taxpayer who files sufficiently late (in the calendar year after the return is due) will also escape inclusion.

It is not unreasonable to suspect that a panel of this sort may exhibit some drift relative to the population as a whole. Although each year's taxpayers in the panel may be representative of the population as a whole, the sampling method may cause a "survivorship" bias or "attrition" among those observations present in more than one year of the panel. Christian and Frischmann (1989) analyzed the first six years of the panel for attrition bias and concluded that the sample of taxpayers present in all those years shows statistically significant differences from population averages. Average income is about 20 percent higher and married couples (specifically, joint filers) are more numerous. Also, compared to a random sample, the fraction of returns for which the primary taxpayer claims an aged exemption (for being sixty-five or older) is lower in the initial year of the panel, rises more rapidly, and is higher in the final year of the panel.

Compared to the tax model files used in Section 3, the critical advantage of the panel data is its longitudinal nature, which allows the researcher the opportunity to identify transitory effects on income. Its principal disadvantage, other than the attrition bias, is the purely random nature of the sample, compared to the stratified random character of the tax model that heavily over-samples upper-income taxpayers.

Table 2 documents that there is a significant amount of mobility in and out of the upper-income classes from year to year, at least for this particular definition of income. In a typical year in the first half of the 1980s, more than 20 percent of taxpayers in the top decile of expanded income had not been in the top decile the previous year. For the top one percentile, the figure rises to 33 percent for 1982 through 1985. Mobility into (and out of) the top classes was extraordinary in 1986, presumably due to the large spurt in capital gains realizations that occurred in anticipation of tax increases due in 1987.

The presence of transitory income means that, in general, those with low income in a snapshot are probably not really as badly off as one

TABLE 2.

Percentage of Those in Top Percentiles of Pre-Tax Expanded Income Who Were Not in That Group in the Previous Year, 1980–1986.

	1980	1981	1982	1983	1984	1985	1986
10%	22	24	21	22	20	23	27
5%	26	28	26	26	24	27	31
1%	28	30	33	33	33	33	40

Source: 1979–1986 Panel of Individual Tax Returns, Balanced Panel Returns only.

year's income suggests and those with high income are probably not as well off as the snapshot suggests. In order to investigate the aggregate magnitude of these effects, I calculate for each taxpayer the average real income over the seven-year period from 1979 to 1985. Although available in the data set, 1986 is excluded from the calculations because of the extraordinary amount of capital gains realizations in that year. I refer to this concept as "time-exposure" income, to contrast it to "snapshot" income.

I purposely distinguish this concept from "permanent" or "lifetime" income. There is a separate literature (e.g., Fitzgerald and Maloney, 1990; Fullerton and Rogers, 1991), which attempts to calculate the inequality of permanent or lifetime income by purging from annual income not only the effect of transitory income but also the life-cycle and intercohort effect. The calculation procedure generally entails first estimating an equation that predicts annual income as a function of variables such as age, education, race, and, if longitudinal data is available, an individual-specific fixed effect, and then calculating the discounted value of projected annual incomes over the expected working life. Using data from 1969 to 1981 from the Panel Study on Income Dynamics, Fitzgerald and Maloney (1990) calculated that, not correcting for intercohort effects, the Gini coefficient for lifetime income was only 1.4 percent lower than that of 1979 income; when intercohort effects were eliminated, the Gini of lifetime income was 19.1 percent lower than that of 1979 income. They also found that the degree to which taxes and transfers reduce inequality is understated by a snapshot, suggesting that the fiscal system does more than smooth household income over the life cycle.

Table 3 illustrates the magnitude of the difference between snapshot and time-exposure income by arraying the latter by the former. There is clear evidence of reversion toward the mean. In 1983 snapshot income classes below $20,000, time-exposure income is greater than 1983 in-

TABLE 3.

Time Exposure Pre-Tax Expanded Income, 1979–1985, by 1983 Pre-Tax Expanded Income Class.

1983 Snapshot expanded income class	Average 1983 expanded income	Average time exposure income, 1979–1985
<0	−22923	34961
0–5000	3063	7395
5–10,000	7764	11168
10–15,000	12586	14244
15–20,000	17553	18967
20–25,000	22372	22830
25–30,000	27501	27477
30–50,000	38596	38128
50–75,000	59360	56640
75–100,000	85229	80276
>100,000	175707	153381

Source: 1979–1986 Panel of Individual Tax Returns, Balanced Panel Returns only.

come. In 1983 classes above $50,000, time-exposure income is clearly less than 1983 income. Between $20,000 and $50,000, 1983 snapshot income on average is close to time-exposure income.

Perhaps the most striking aspect of Table 3 is the starkly different pictures one gets of the lowest income class. The average time-exposure income of those who, in 1983, had negative expanded AGI, was $34,961. It has long been understood that those with negative income for tax purposes in a given year are often not truly poor, but this table shows just how important that phenomenon is. Not only are these people not poor, but on average they are solidly middle class.

B. Income Inequality

There have been several studies of the effect of extending the accounting period on measured inequality (e.g. Shorrocks, 1978a; and Benus and Morgan, 1975). The general conclusion, based on comparisons of annual measures of inequality to inequality measured over two or more years, has been that a longer accounting period reduces inequality very little. That conclusion must, though, be tempered by the tendency for relative inequality to increase as cohorts of individuals get older.

Table 4 compares the distribution of pre-tax expanded income and some of its components (ordered by income, not the component itself) when computed from snapshots and a time exposure; all columns sum to 100. For the columns headed SA, the figures shown are the simple average of the seven years' results when taxpayers are arranged by that

TABLE 4.

Distribution of Snapshot Average Time-Exposure Pre-Tax Expanded Income, 1979–1985, and Some Components, by Expanded Income Percentiles.

Expanded income percentile	Expanded income		Wages & salaries		Interest & dividends		Business (Sch. C)	
	SA	TE	SA	TE	SA	TE	SA	TE
0–10	0.96	1.83	1.54	2.09	3.12	3.27	0.22	2.90
10–20	3.21	3.72	2.93	3.57	5.18	4.34	3.56	3.91
20–30	4.56	4.87	4.45	5.01	5.61	5.21	4.19	4.46
30–40	5.84	6.07	5.81	6.01	6.33	6.34	5.85	7.52
40–50	7.25	7.42	7.28	7.52	7.02	6.68	8.07	7.62
50–60	8.91	8.94	9.54	9.47	6.00	5.54	9.60	9.45
60–70	10.71	10.62	11.86	11.71	5.98	5.78	7.69	7.82
70–80	12.81	12.57	13.97	13.54	8.20	8.57	8.99	9.70
80–90	15.80	15.47	17.12	16.31	11.74	10.97	12.33	14.66
90–95	10.02	9.80	10.42	10.18	8.88	9.66	11.22	5.72
95–99	11.55	11.06	10.12	9.58	15.66	18.01	23.86	23.71
99–100	8.39	7.64	4.98	5.02	16.30	15.61	4.43	2.54

Percentile	Capital gains		Tax liability	
	SA	TE	SA	TE
0–10	1.88	2.16	0.28	0.72
10–20	0.67	1.04	1.16	1.79
20–30	0.68	1.32	2.37	2.89
30–40	1.15	1.49	3.64	3.99
40–50	2.09	2.13	5.10	5.40
50–60	1.81	2.31	6.99	7.22
60–70	1.84	5.03	8.93	9.03
70–80	4.18	5.84	11.52	11.26
80–90	6.67	7.84	15.99	15.73
90–95	6.73	8.18	11.48	11.32
95–99	20.47	19.00	16.26	15.43
99–100	51.84	43.67	16.29	15.23

Source: 1979–1986 Panel of Individual Tax Returns, Balanced Panel Returns only.

year's expanded income. Thus, for example, the 0.96 in the first row of the first column means that, averaged over 1979 to 1985, 0.96 percent of total snapshot expanded income for that year is received by the lowest 10 percent of expanded income earners in that year. For the columns headed TE, the taxpayers are arranged by time-exposure income, so that 1.83 percent of time-exposure income is received by the lowest 10 percent of taxpayers when ranked by time-exposure income.

Table 4 reveals that, although the distribution based on time-exposure income is less skewed than the average distribution based on snapshots, the difference is not striking. First consider the fraction of income earned by the top percentiles as an indicator of income distribution skewness. In the snapshot average, the top 1 percent, 5 percent, and 10 percent of income earners receive 8.39 percent, 19.94 percent, and 29.96 percent of income. For 1979–1985 time-exposure income, these classes receive 7.64 percent, 18.70 percent, and 28.50 percent of income, respectively. Another notable difference is the greater shares of income going to the lower income classes in time-exposure income (5.55 percent versus 4.17 percent for the bottom two deciles), reflecting the fact that a significant fraction of low incomes in a snapshot reflect transitory negative components.

One other fact worth noting now, and worth returning to in Section V, is the large difference in measured inequality for a snapshot of a random sample of taxpayers and a snapshot of only those taxpayers who appear in all years of the panel. For example, in 1984, the Gini of before-tax income for the former is 0.524 compared to 0.422 for those who appear in all years of the panel. The large decline is due to the fact that it is predominantly low-income taxpayers who do not appear in all years, and thus are dropped from the "balanced" panel of returns that includes only those who filed a timely return in each year from 1979 to 1986. This results in a lower measure of inequality. Thus it is important to distinguish not only between a snapshot and a time-exposure picture of the income distribution, but also between snapshots of all returns filed in a year and a snapshot of all returns filed in a year by people who file in eight consecutive years.

C. Time-Exposure vs. Snapshot Sources of Income

It is also instructive to compare the snapshot and time-exposure distributions of sources of income. First focus on the top 1 percent of income earners in Table 4. The average of the snapshot distribution from the balanced panel reveals that 51.84 percent of all capital gains are received by this group; by time-exposure income this figure falls to 43.67 percent. Thus a snapshot overstates the extent to which capital gains are received by high-income individuals. Nevertheless, by either measure this is largely a phenomenon of the upper-income classes.[6]

For interest and dividends, the story is quite different. Focusing on the top 5 percent of income earners, there is a greater concentration among

---

[6] This is consistent with other evidence that shows that most capital gains are realized by individuals who regularly have realizations. See Slemrod, Kalambokidis, and Shobe (1989).

the highest-income classes using time-exposure compared to snapshot distributions—33.62 percent versus 31.96 percent. The story here is that high interest and dividends really do characterize the permanently well-off taxpayers, and a snapshot obscures the picture by replacing some of these taxpayers with others who have temporarily high income. For the top 1 percent of income, the time-exposure concentration is slightly lower than the snapshot average concentration, but the difference is much less marked than for capital gains, 15.61 percent compared to 16.31 percent.

Table 5 shows, by percentile class, some sources of expanded income for an average of 1979 to 1985 snapshots and time-exposure income, respectively. Thus in this table the rows of SA figures and TE figures would each sum to 100 if all sources were included. Many of the same patterns of Table 4 appear here. The final columns, which portray tax liability as a fraction of pre-tax expanded income, are worth noting. Based on time-exposure income, the average tax burden continually increases with income and ranges from 6.07 percent for the lowest income class to 30.70 percent for the highest. In contrast, based on an average of snapshots, the lowest income classes have a lower average tax burden. The average tax liability of the highest class is also slightly lower in snapshots compared to time-exposure income, 29.99 percent as compared to 30.70 percent.

V. LONG-TERM TRENDS FROM A TIME-EXPOSURE PERSPECTIVE

Section III of this paper showed that snapshots of annual tax return data reveal a nearly continual increase in pre-tax income inequality between 1972 and 1988, with tax liability playing a small, or even negative, role in offsetting that trend. Section IV argued that snapshots of the 1980s overstate slightly the inequality of time-exposure income, a conceptually more appealing measure of well-being.

In this section I attempt to draw the two strands of this research together in order to answer the following type of question: Does comparing snapshots of 1972 and 1988 misstate the true change in inequality because of a change in the accuracy of a snapshot as a measure of time-exposure income? In particular I investigate the intriguing hypothesis that because of increased mobility, the increase in snapshot inequality overstates the increase in time-exposure inequality.

To address these issues I make use of an earlier panel of tax returns that spans the years 1967 to 1973. As for the 1979 to 1986 panel, the 1967 to 1973 data set was created by drawing all tax returns whose primary

TABLE 5.

Breakdown of Expanded Income, 1979–1985, into Sources of Income, by Percentile.

Expanded income percentile	Wages & salaries		Interest & dividends		Business (Sch. C)	
	SA	TE	SA	TE	SA	TE
0–10	134.83	94.29	31.10	15.93	0.52	4.73
10–20	75.75	79.43	14.36	10.43	3.32	3.14
20–30	80.68	85.05	10.81	9.57	2.75	2.73
30–40	82.18	81.94	9.62	9.34	2.94	3.70
40–50	83.09	83.73	8.74	8.04	3.32	3.06
50–60	88.48	87.56	6.03	5.53	3.18	3.15
60–70	91.59	91.12	5.01	4.86	2.12	2.20
70–80	90.21	89.05	5.65	6.09	2.05	2.30
80–90	89.57	87.17	6.66	6.33	2.37	2.83
90–95	85.98	85.86	7.87	8.80	3.35	1.74
95–99	72.52	71.57	12.13	14.53	6.16	6.39
99–100	49.32	54.32	17.35	18.24	1.75	0.99
TOTAL	82.69	82.67	8.91	8.93	2.98	2.98

Percentile	Capital Gains		Tax Liability	
	SA	TE	SA	TE
0–10	8.81	4.68	4.61	6.07
10–20	0.71	1.11	5.50	7.41
20–30	0.55	1.08	7.97	9.15
30–40	0.70	0.97	9.59	10.14
40–50	1.07	1.14	10.83	11.21
50–60	0.79	1.03	12.07	12.44
60–70	0.61	1.88	12.84	13.09
70–80	1.21	1.84	13.86	13.79
80–90	1.58	2.01	15.59	15.66
90–95	2.56	3.30	17.64	17.78
95–99	6.59	6.80	21.71	21.48
99–100	24.56	22.64	29.99	30.70
Total	3.92	3.96	15.41	15.40

Source: 1979–1986 Panel of Individual Tax Returns, Balanced Panel Returns only.

taxpayer had certain four-digit social security number endings. This procedure results in a random sample of taxpayers for any given year, but the sample of taxpayers for which there is a tax return in each of the seven years, the focus of our study, is not a random sample, and will exhibit the same sort of attrition biases discussed above. This attrition

TABLE 6.

*Percentage of Those in Top Percentiles of Expanded Income Who Were
Not in that Group in the Previous Year, 1968–1973.*

	1968	1969	1970	1971	1972	1973
10%	20	24	23	20	19	21
5%	21	24	24	23	22	23
1%	20	20	24	25	24	23

Source: 1979–1986 Panel of Individual Tax Returns, Balanced Panel Returns only.

bias is particularly troubling in this context, as taxpayers whose incomes
are more subject to downward mobility are more likely to be excluded
from the sample.

I look first directly at a simple indicator of income mobility. Table 6
reproduces Table 2 for the 1967 to 1973 period, showing the percentage
of those in the top 1, 5, and 10 percentiles that were not in that group in
the previous year. There are clear differences between the two periods,
especially for the top 1 percent and 5 percent groups. Over the 1968 to
1973 period, an average of 22.8 percent of those in the top 5 percent had
not been in that group the year before; for the 1980 to 1986 period that
figure rises to 26.9 percent (26.2 percent if 1986 is excluded). The difference is even larger for the top 1 percent of taxpayers. The average fraction who had not been among the top 1 percent in the previous year was
22.7 percent between 1968 and 1973; it increased to 32.9 percent between
1980 and 1986 (31.7 percent excluding 1986).

Thus there is some evidence that income mobility—at least among the
highest income groups—increased between 1967 and 1973 and 1979 and
1986. It is, therefore, conceivable that some of the increase in snapshot
inequality between these two periods does not correspond to an increase
in inequality of a more permanent notion of income.

The first two columns of Table 7 address this issue by comparing the
distribution of time-exposure income in the 1967 to 1973 panel to that of
time-exposure income in the 1979 to 1985 period. In the later period the
fraction of expanded income received by the poorest half of the population declined significantly, from 25.69 percent to 23.90 percent. The
mirror image of this trend is an increase in the share of income earned by
the top half, with one notable exception. The share of expanded income
received by the top 1 percent declines from 10.42 percent to 7.64 percent
between the two periods. Thus, based on these figures in Table 7, the
characterization that "the poor got poorer and the rich got richer" must
be amended to add "except for the very rich." The amendment regard-

TABLE 7.
Comparison of Inequality Measures for Before-Tax Time-Exposure Income Using the 1967–1973 Panel and the 1979–1985 Panel.

Percentile	1967–1973	1979–1985	1970–1973	1982–1985
0–10	2.23	1.83	2.19	1.62
10–20	3.96	3.72	4.06	3.61
20–30	5.30	4.87	5.43	4.85
30–40	6.53	6.06	6.60	6.01
40–50	7.65	7.42	7.84	7.31
50–60	8.77	8.94	9.00	8.90
60–70	10.07	10.62	10.31	10.66
70–80	11.62	12.57	11.93	12.69
80–90	14.00	15.47	14.43	15.56
90–95	8.89	9.80	9.14	9.94
95–99	10.56	11.06	10.75	11.45
99–100	10.42	7.64	8.26	7.40
	100	100	100	100
Before-Tax Gini	.373	.390	.361	.397
After-Tax Gini	.347	.363	.335	.373

Source: 1967–1973 and 1979–1986 Panel of Individual Tax Returns, Balanced Panel Returns only.

ing the very rich is reflected in the Gini summary measure of inequality, which between these two periods increased from 0.373 to only 0.390, not nearly as large an increase as one might expect based on the snapshots of inequality discussed in Section III of this paper.

Compared to the results of Table 1, the numbers in Table 7 might seem to suggest that much of the increase in inequality over the past two decades is an artifact of comparing snapshots of distributions, and that in particular the concentration of income in the highest income classes has been overstated. This conclusion is not warranted.

The principal reason for the discrepancy is that the first three years of the 1967 to 1973 period apparently predate the secular increase in inequality. In fact, the snapshot Gini coefficients from the balanced panel for 1967 and 1968 are higher than those of nearly any other year in either panel.[7] Table 8 presents the Gini coefficients for each year of the two panels (excluding 1986 for the later panel, so that each panel contains

---

[7] The measured Gini coefficient for 1968 is particularly high due to the presence in the sample of one return with a capital gain equal to more than 4 percent of the total income of all taxpayers in that year's sample. The actual snapshot inequality in 1969, and possibly 1968, is due in part to the large amount of capital gains realizations in this year in anticipation of increased effective capital gains taxes, beginning in 1970. In this respect 1969 is like 1986. See Slemrod and Feldstein (1978).

TABLE 8.
Gini Coefficients and Decomposition of Pre-Tax Time-Exposure Expanded Income, 1967–1973 and 1979–1985.

| | 1967–1973 | | | | 1979–1985 | | |
	Gini	Share	Rho		Gini	Share	Rho
Time-Exposure Income	.373			Time-Exposure Income	.390		
1967	.431	.126	.896	1979	.425	.135	.897
1968	.468	.148	.940	1980	.433	.142	.934
1969	.402	.141	.942	1981	.417	.142	.944
1970	.381	.140	.945	1982	.410	.139	.950
1971	.383	.142	.937	1983	.418	.141	.935
1972	.383	.149	.924	1984	.422	.148	.922
1973	.381	.153	.882	1985	.422	.154	.903

Source: 1967–1973 and 1979–1986 Panel of Individual Tax Returns, Balanced Panel Returns only.

seven years), as well as a Gini decomposition of time-exposure income into its component years. The values of rho, which indicate the variability of income over time, are not clearly different across the two periods. A more formal comparison uses the measure of income mobility proposed by Shorrocks (1978b), the ratio of (what I call) time-exposure inequality to a weighted average of annual measures of inequality, where the weights are the share of annual income in aggregate time-exposure income. This comes to 0.9229 for 1967 to 1973 and 0.9260 for 1979 to 1985, indicating a slight decline in income mobility.

The final two columns of Table 6 confirm the importance of 1967 to 1969 for the conclusion that inequality did not increase much between the two panel periods. These columns recalculate the distribution of before-tax time-exposure expanded income, where time-exposure income is calculated using only 1970 to 1973 for the earlier panel and only 1982 to 1985 for the later panel. The comparison of four-year time-exposure incomes shows that there is a much less noticeable difference in the concentration of incomes at the top. The increase in the Gini coefficient of both pre-tax and after-tax income is about twice as large as is evident when comparing the seven-year panels. The fact that the increase in inequality between the two periods is less than one would have guessed from Table 1 is primarily due to the difference in the samples studied; Table 1 refers to the entire taxpaying population, while Tables 6 and 7 refer only to those taxpayers who filed returns in each of several years.

Thus it appears that there was no significant change between 1967 and

1973 and 1979 and 1985 in the degree to which snapshots overestimate the inequality in time-exposure income. The small increase in the Gini coefficient of time-exposure income predominantly reflects the fact that the earlier period includes the high inequality years of 1967 through 1969.

VI. CONCLUSIONS AND CAVEATS

The principal conclusions from this study can be summarized as follows:

1. Based on annual tax return data, the inequality of pre-tax income has been increasing steadily between 1972 and 1988. The major factor in this trend has been the increasing inequality in the distribution of wages and salaries.
2. Assuming exogenous pre-tax incomes, income taxation slightly decreases inequality. Overall it has neither stemmed nor contributed significantly to the general trend. Since 1980 the contribution of the income tax to decreasing inequality has declined slightly.
3. Replacing annual income with "time-exposure" income, defined as average real income over the whole period, does not significantly reduce the measured degree of inequality in the 1979 to 1985 period, although the fraction of income received by the lowest decile does increase substantially. This procedure does, though, reduce the contribution to inequality of certain sources of income such as capital gains and increase the contribution of other sources such as interest and dividends.
4. There is only a slight increase between the 1967 to 1973 and 1979 to 1985 periods in the inequality of time-exposure income, a finding apparently at odds with the measures of snapshot inequality. Much of the discrepancy is, however, due to the inclusion in the former period of the relatively high inequality years between 1967 and 1969. There is no systematic evidence that the comparison of snapshots between the two periods overstates the growth of inequality of a more permanent notion of income.

Because all of these conclusions are based on an examination of tax return data, several important caveats apply. The most important is that, because households with income below a filing threshold need not file a return, the distribution of taxpayers in any snapshot will omit a significant fraction of the lower tail of the distribution of household income. Moreover, because the real filing threshold is not constant over time, the extent of taxpayers omitted from the snapshot changes. Thus, conclusions 1 and 2 pertain to the universe of taxpayers, and not necessarily to the universe of all households.

An additional caveat applies to conclusions 3 and 4, which are based on distributions of snapshots and time exposures. These comparisons are based on a subset of taxpayers—those who filed returns in each of a number of consecutive years. Because this sampling criterion will tend to exclude taxpayers whose income occasionally falls below the filing threshold, it will likely understate the amount of snapshot income mobility. Furthermore, because the real filing thresholds change, the extent of this effect may be different across the two panels studied here.

These caveats are meant to be taken seriously. They suggest that further research should focus on the extent to which the trends in the distributions of income and income sources among taxpayers reflect accurately the trends in the distribution for all households, and on the degree to which income mobility is misstated by ignoring taxpayers who do not regularly file returns.

Policy decisions affecting the distribution of income cannot, alas, await these desirable refinements to the techniques employed here. Much analysis of alternative tax policies focuses solely on the taxpaying population, without placing the results into the larger context of all households. Thus it is valuable to know which kinds of conclusions about taxation and inequality based on snapshots are likely to apply to a more permanent notion of income. This paper is a first step in that direction.

REFERENCES

Beach, Charles (1989). "Dollars and Dreams: A Reduced Middle Class—Alternative Explanations," *The Journal of Human Resources* 24(1).

Benus, J., and J. N. Morgan (1975). "Time Period, Unit of Analysis and Income Concept in the Analysis of Income Distribution." In *The Personal Distributions of Income and Wealth.* J. D. Smith, ed. New York: National Bureau of Economic Research.

Christian, Charles W., and Peter J. Frischmann (1989). "Attrition in the Statistics of Income Panel of Individual Returns," *National Tax Journal*, 62(4), December. 495–501.

Danziger, Sheldon, Peter Gottschalk, and Eugene Smolensky (1989). "How the Rich Have Fared, 1973–1987," *American Economic Review* 79, 310–314.

Duncan, Greg J., Timothy M. Smeeding, and Willard Rodgers (1991). "W(h)ither the Middle Class? A Dynamic View." Prepared for the Levy Institute Conference on Income Inequality, Bard College, June 18–20.

Fitzgerald, John and Tim Maloney (1990). "The Impact of Federal Income Taxes and Cash Transfers on the Distribution of Lifetime Household Income, 1969–81." *Public Finance Quarterly* 18 (2), April, 182–197.

Fullerton, Don, and Diane Lim Rogers (1991). *Who Bears the Lifetime Tax Burden?* Manuscript prepared for the Brookings Institution.

Gramlich, Edward, Richard Kasten, and Frank Sammartino (1991). "Growing Inequality in the 1980's: The Role of Taxes and Transfers." In *Increasing Income Inequality: What Matters and What Doesn't.* S. Danziger and P. Gottschalk, eds. New York: Russell Sage Foundation.

Karoly, L. A. (1991). "The Trend in Inequality Among Families, Individuals, and Workers in the United States: A Twenty-Five Year Perspective." In *Increasing Income Inequality: What Matters and What Doesn't.* S. Danziger and P. Gottschalk, eds. New York: Russell Sage Foundation.

Lerman, Robert I., and Shlomo Yitzhaki (1985). "Income Inequality Effects by Income Source: A New Approach and Applications to the United States." *Review of Economics and Statistics* 47, February, 151–155.

Levy, Frank (1987). *Dollars and Dreams: The Changing American Income Distribution.* New York: Russell Sage.

Levy, Frank, and Richard J. Murname (1991). "Earnings Levels and Earnings Inequality: A Review of Recent Trends and Proposed Explanations." University of Maryland, Unpublished manuscript, February.

Lindsey, Lawrence (1990). *The Growth Experiment.* New York: Basic Books.

Poterba, James M. (1989). "Lifetime Incidence and the Distributional Burden of Excise Taxes." *American Economic Review* 79 (2) May, 325–330.

Shorrocks, Anthony F. (1978a). "Income Inequality and Income Mobility." *Journal of Economic Theory* 19, 376–393.

———— (1978b). "Income Stability in the United States," London School of Economics, Unpublished manuscript, December.

Slemrod, Joel (1983). "Do We Know How Progressive the Income Tax System Should Be?" *National Tax Journal* September. 36, 361–369.

Slemrod, Joel, and Martin Feldstein (1978). "The Lock-In Effect of the Capital Gains Tax: Some Time-Series Evidence." *Tax Notes* August. 134–135.

Slemrod, Joel, Laura Kalambokidis, and William Shobe (1989). "Who Realizes Capital Gains?" *Tax Notes* October 23. 494–495.

Varian, Hal (1980). "Redistributive Taxation as Social Insurance." *Journal of Public Economics* 14, 49–68.

SOCIAL SECURITY AND MEDICARE POLICY FROM THE PERSPECTIVE OF GENERATIONAL ACCOUNTING

Alan J. Auerbach
University of Pennsylvania and NBER

Jagadeesh Gokhale
Federal Reserve Bank of Cleveland

Laurence J. Kotlikoff
Boston University and NBER

EXECUTIVE SUMMARY

Our previous studies (Auerbach, Gokhale, and Kotlikoff, 1991 and 1992) and Kotlikoff (1992) introduced the concept of "generational account-ing," a method of determining how the burden of fiscal policy falls on different generations. It found that fiscal policy in the United States is out of balance, in terms of projected generational burdens. This means that either current generations will bear a larger share (than we project under current law) of the burden of the government's spending or that future generations will have to pay, on average, at least 21 percent more,

This paper has been prepared for the annual NBER conference on Tax Policy and the Economy, Washington D.C., November 1991. Sections of this paper draw on Auerbach, Gokhale, and Kotlikoff (1991, 1992) and Kotlikoff (1992).

on a growth-adjusted basis, than will those generations who have just been born.

These conclusions were based on relatively optimistic assumptions about the path of social security and Medicare policies, namely that the accumulation of a social security trust fund would continue and that Medicare costs would not rise as a share of GNP. In this paper, we simulate the effects of realistic alternative paths for social security and Medicare. Our results suggest that such alternative policies could greatly increase the imbalance in generational policy, making not only future generations pay significantly more, but current young Americans as well. For example, continued expansion of Medicare in this decade alone could double the 21 percent imbalance figure if the bill for this Medicare growth is shifted primarily to future generations.

I. INTRODUCTION

Recent years have witnessed a growing skepticism about the use of the fiscal deficit to gauge the stance of economic policy. Many economists as well as noneconomists are questioning whether a single number, that relates primarily to the government's current cash flow, is the kind of measure needed to understand the longer term effects of fiscal policy on saving, investment, and growth. They also ask whether the deficit can tell us how we are treating different generations, both those currently alive and those yet to come. Doubts about the deficit have been accentuated by the aging of the U.S. population, with its attendant increase in the number of retirees dependent on workers for pay-as-you-go spending and transfer programs.

In recognition of these concerns about the demographic transition, the U.S. federal government began, in 1983, to accumulate a large social security trust fund to help finance the social security benefits of the "baby boom" generation. But this break with short-term, pay-as-you-go financing also raised new questions about using the unified federal deficit, which includes social security, as a measure of fiscal policy. If funds for the future need to be accumulated by the social security system, then shouldn't such accumulations be excluded from the overall deficit measure? The federal government's response, as expressed in the 1990 budget agreement, has been to exclude social security from future calculations of the deficit. This has not prevented public discussion of the deficit inclusive of social security. Nor has it put to rest the concern that government spending is now larger and will continue to be larger and that taxes are now smaller and will continue to be smaller than they would in the absence of the social security surpluses; that is, it has not put to rest the concern that the federal government is "using" the large pay-as-you-go social security surpluses to offset large on-budget deficits.

This is but one example of the ambiguity of the deficit and the deficiency of any single deficit measure as a gauge of the fiscal burden faced by different generations. Although one response to this deficiency has been to construct different deficits for different purposes, such constructs are clearly ad hoc in nature and require continual "refinements" to prevent perverse results. For example, if the social security system is excluded from the budget for deficit purposes, how does one deal with changes in income taxes that are induced by changes in social security taxes? Should such changes in off-budget taxes be permitted to alter the on-budget deficit?

The key economic question associated with fiscal deficits is this: Which generation will pay for what the government spends? No version of the government's budget deficit provides this information. As we discuss later, an increase in the deficit does not necessarily signal a shift in the fiscal burden to future generations. Moreover, policies that dramatically alter the intergenerational distribution of fiscal burdens may do so without inducing any change whatsoever in the measured deficit.

In earlier papers (Auerbach, Gokhale, and Kotlikoff, 1991 and 1992) and in a book (Kotlikoff, 1992), we developed an alternative to the deficit—generational accounting—and showed how this new approach could be used to assess fiscal policy and its distributional impact with respect to different generations. Our previous analysis stressed that generational accounts are quite informative about the effects of changes in tax and transfer policies on the burdens of different generations. This paper uses generational accounting to analyze potential changes in the federal government's most important transfer program, the Old Age Survivors, Disability, and Health Insurance (OASDHI), which includes the old-age Social Security pension system and Medicare. This component of the federal budget has grown much more rapidly than other components in recent years. If current trends continue, OASDHI will continue to grow relative to the economy due to the increasing share of the elderly in the population and the rapid increase in real medical costs.

Before turning to such policy analysis, we briefly review the generational accounting methodology, which is discussed more fully in Auerbach, Gokhale, and Kotlikoff (1991, 1992).

II. THE GENERATIONAL ACCOUNTING APPROACH

The basic idea behind generational accounting is that generations currently alive and those yet to be born must pay for the time-path of the government's expenditures on goods and services less the external resources the government has to cover these expenditures (its net wealth). This is the government's intertemporal budget constraint. The constraint reminds us of the zero-sum nature of paying for the government's expenditures; if generations currently alive pay less, generations yet to come will be forced to pay more. It also reminds us that changes in fiscal policy today are likely to necessitate changes in the future. We express the government's intertemporal budget constraint in present value, with the initial value of government liabilities and the present value of future spending being equal to the sum of the present values of each generation's burden. Regardless of the year in which such burdens are imposed, emphasizing the present value burdens of different generations neutralizes the timing problems inherent in annual deficit measures, and allows us to summarize in a compact form the likely effects of fiscal policy on individuals through time.

The analysis is forward-looking in that it calculates only the future fiscal burdens that each generation faces. Because we are interested in the issue of generational imbalance in fiscal policy, we treat current and future generations separately when analyzing a particular fiscal policy path. For current generations, we calculate the burden under the particular fiscal scenario. For future generations, we calculate the total present value of payments required to balance the government's intertemporal budget constraint. One cannot say how this aggregate burden on future generations will be distributed across these future generations. For purposes of illustrating the size of the burden likely to be imposed on future generations relative to that likely to be imposed on current generations, we assume that the burden on each successive future generation remains fixed as a fraction of the lifetime income of that generation; that is, the absolute fiscal burden of successive generations grows at the rate of growth of their lifetime incomes, which we take to be the rate of growth of productivity.

To calculate the burden faced by a member of an existing generation, we first project the net payments to the government in each future year for a representative member of that generation (distinguishing males and females) and then take the present value of such payments. By net payments we mean all taxes paid to, less all transfers received from, government at the federal, state, and local levels. Payments include not only direct taxes such as income and property taxes, but also indirect business taxes, corporate taxes, and seignorage. Transfers include Medicare, Medicaid, Food Stamps, Social Security Benefits, and so on.

The present value calculation for each representative individual discounts future payments not only for interest, but also mortality: An individual's future burden is reduced by the probability that he or she will not be alive when that burden occurs. Given our assumption that members of each generation (distinguished only by sex) face the same survival probabilities, multiplying individual payments in each year by the generation's projected surviving population for that year provides a measure of that generation's payment, the separate components of which are benchmarked to aggregates from the National Income and Product Accounts.

Once burdens for current generations have been calculated, those faced by future generations are estimated as a residual, based on the fiscal balance requirement and the assumption that the remaining fiscal burden be borne proportionally. Policy changes affect the projected net payments faced by current generations and, through the fiscal balance requirement, the burden on future generations as well.

Because the accounts are forward-looking, they do not consider the net payments made in the past. The present value of future net payments, which are positive for young and middle-aged existing generations, are negative for older generations, who are largely retired and facing lower labor income taxes while at the same time receiving social security benefits and Medicare. Thus, the level of an existing generation's account does not indicate how well or poorly that generation has fared at the hands of the government. We therefore focus on the changes in each generation's account that are induced by alternative policies.

III. CONSTRUCTION OF GENERATIONAL ACCOUNTS

The construction of generational accounts is a two-step process. The first step entails projecting each currently living generation's average taxes less transfers in each future year during which at least some members of the generation will be alive. The second step converts these projected average net tax payments into a present value using an assumed discount rate and taking into account the probability that the generations' members will be alive in each of the future years (i.e., actuarial discounting for both mortality and interest).

In projecting each currently living generation's taxes and transfers, we consider first their taxes and transfers in the base year, in this case, 1989. The totals of the different taxes and transfers in the base year are those reported by the National Income and Product Accounts. As described in detail in Auerbach, Gokhale, and Kotlikoff (1991), these totals of base year taxes and transfers are distributed to the different generations according to their ages and sexes based on cross-section survey data. These data include the Bureau of the Census' Survey of Income and Plan Participation and the Bureau of Labor Statistics' Survey of Consumer Expenditures. The distribution of future taxes and transfers by age and sex is assumed to equal that in the current year with adjustments for growth and projected changes in policy.

Because the government already forecasts the totals of its various taxes and transfers for many years ahead, the additional work involved in generational accounting is primarily in allocating these projected totals by age and sex. Thus, although there are a few additional elements and the requisite projections extend farther into the future, generational accounting uses mostly the same numbers the government uses, only in a different manner.

The calculations presented here assume a 6.00 percent real rate of discount and a productivity growth rate of 0.75 percent. The rate of productivity growth is based on recent U.S. experience. The discount rate is higher than the rate of return on government obligations, reflecting the fact that future government receipts and expenditures are risky.[1] The estimates also incorporate the mortality probabilities embedded in the Social Security Administration's projections of the U.S. population by age and sex. As discussed in Auerbach, Gokhale, and Kotlikoff (1991), the absolute value of the generational accounts is sensitive to the choice of rates of discount and growth as well as rates of birth and death. But for many of the questions of interest, such as the fiscal burden being imposed on future generations relative to that being shouldered by current generations, the results are quite robust to reasonable departures from baseline assumptions.

As mentioned, inferring the fiscal burden on future generations requires not only knowing the sum total of generational accounts of current generations, but also the projected present value of the government's expenditures on goods and services as well as the government's initial net wealth position. As described in Auerbach, Gokhale, and Kotlikoff (1991), the government's net wealth is estimated in a manner consistent with the government sector deficit reported in the National Income Accounts. The

---

[1] As we discussed in our 1991 paper, the appropriate discount rate to use depends on the risk characteristics of the flows being discounted. (A similar point has been made by Bohn, 1991). If government receipts and expenditures were roughly proportional to aggregate fluctuations in income, then the private sector discount rate, measured by the real before-tax rate of return, would seem the appropriate discount rate to use. We use a somewhat lower rate to reflect the existence of countercyclical government policy. In principle, one would also discount separate components of expenditures and net receipts using different rates.

present value of government expenditures is calculated by projecting current expenditures into the future taking into account those expenditure elements that are sensitive to the demographic structure. For example, our projections take into account the decline in per capita spending on education that is likely to arise as the school-age population declines relative to the total population.

Our baseline generational accounts reflect policy as of 1989 (prior to the 1990 budget agreement). They show that a newborn male faced a net payment to the government of $73,700, reflecting present values of $85,300 of tax payments and $11,600 of transfers received. For females, the comparable figures are $36,400 in net present value, comprising $54,700 in taxes and $18,300 in transfers. The lower taxes for females primarily reflect their lower rate of labor force participation, and hence lower income and payroll taxes. The higher transfers reflect greater female longevity and the concentration of female-headed households in circumstances of poverty. Together, Medicare and social security account for nearly half of all transfers received by males, and over a third of those received by females.

Based on our estimates of initial government wealth and the projections of the effects of this baseline fiscal policy on existing generations, we find that, as of 1989, generational policy was out of balance in the sense that the fiscal burden on future generations was 21 percent larger than that on 1989 male and female newborns, who are assumed to fall under the current policy regime. As the net lifetime payments newborns are projected to make represent almost 40 percent of their lifetime incomes, this imbalance in generational policy translates into an added burden of nearly one tenth of the income of members of future generations.

An alternative way of measuring how far the current regime is out of generational balance is the change in any particular fiscal instrument that would be necessary to bring this 21 percent excess to zero—to make the "new" current policy sustainable without further adjustment. Our calculations suggest that an immediate and permanent increase in the average income tax rate of 5.3 percent (just under 1 percentage point) would suffice. If, instead, payroll taxes were used to equalize the burden, they would have to rise by 7.8 percent, or about 1 percentage point. Alternatively, a rise in sales taxes of 10.2 percent (just over 1 percentage point) or a 14.3 percent rise (nearly 4 percentage points) in capital income taxes would be required. Although any of these fiscal instruments (or many others) could be used to provide intergenerational balance, each policy change would lead to a different burden on current and future generations. The most favorable to the young and future generations are sales taxes, more of which would be paid by older individuals. At the other extreme, not surprisingly, are payroll taxes. Hence, generational balance may be achieved with a range of impacts on particular generations.[2]

IV. GENERATIONAL ACCOUNTING AND DEFICITS

The usefulness of generational accounting is immediately clear when one compares the effects of specific fiscal polices on deficits and generational accounts. Policies that change the pattern of generational burdens need not affect the deficit, while other policies may change the deficit without affecting the pattern of generational burdens. This is illustrated by Table 1 (reprinted by permission from Kotlikoff 1992), which present simulations of the effects of four different, but not unusual, policies.

The first of these policies is a five-year, 20 percent reduction in the average federal income tax rate, with the tax rate increased above its initial value after five years to maintain a constant debt-to-GNP ratio. This policy would raise the deficit and shift the fiscal burden to young and future generations, not a surprising result. The second policy—an immediate and permanent 20 percent increase in social security retirement and disability benefits financed on a pay-as-you-go basis by increases in payroll taxes—would induce a quite similar shifting of fiscal burdens without any change in the time path of measured deficits (including or excluding the social security system). The third policy involves an equal revenue switch in tax structure, a permanent 30 percent cut in payroll taxes financed by increased sales taxes, which, again, shifts generational burdens without changing the deficit.

The final policy illustrated in Table 1 involves the elimination of the discount that presently exists in the price of existing assets as a result of investment incentives. Removing this discount (as would be accomplished by extending the tax treatment of new assets to existing assets) is essentially a windfall grant to owners of existing capital. We assume in the simulation that this grant is paid for by a permanent increase in capital income tax rates, a policy shift that transfers resources from the young (who, on average, have not yet accumulated significant wealth) to the old (who, on average, have).

As the simulations in this section indicate, the generational effects of a variety of realistic policies cannot be determined by looking at deficits. We turn now to an examination of several social security and Medicare policies that may actually be adopted through time.

[2] See Auerbach, Gokhale, and Kotlikoff (1992) for further discussion.

TABLE 1.

Changes in Generational Accounts Arising from Four Hypothetical
Policies (present value, thousands of dollars).

	5-year tax cut	20 percent social security benefit increase	Shifting from payroll to sales and excise taxes	Eliminating investment incentives
Males				
Ages				
0	1.9	2.7	1.0	0.9
10	3.2	3.9	−1.3	1.5
20	2.2	5.5	−6.5	2.3
30	−0.3	5.2	−8.8	2.1
40	−2.7	2.4	−7.5	0.2
50	−4.4	−2.7	−3.8	−2.5
60	−5.0	−10.2	0.7	−4.7
70	−2.6	−11.9	3.4	−5.0
80	−1.6	−7.3	2.8	−4.0
Future generations	1.9	3.1	0.4	0.2
Females				
Ages				
0	1.0	1.0	3.5	0.4
10	1.7	1.5	3.2	0.6
20	0.7	1.9	1.5	0.8
30	−0.2	0.9	1.8	1.2
40	−1.0	−1.0	2.4	0.6
50	−1.9	−4.5	3.1	−0.5
60	−2.1	−10.0	3.9	−1.8
70	−1.5	−11.0	3.9	−2.4
80	−0.9	−7.5	2.8	−2.4
Future generations	1.0	1.1	3.8	0.1

V. THE GENERATIONAL IMPACTS OF SOCIAL POLICIES

A. Social Security's OASDI Program

We first consider policies to alter the structure of the OASDI (non-Medicare) portion of the social security system. As a result of the increases in payroll taxes mandated by the 1983 changes, this program has in recent years been running large cash flow surpluses of roughly 100 billion dollars per year. Although these accumulations were planned to help offset benefit payments in the decades to come, their existence, combined with historically high payroll tax rates, has lent force to arguments for reducing payroll taxes. Cutting payroll taxes is not, in itself, a full description of a fiscal policy, however; payroll tax cuts alone would cause a violation of the government's fiscal balance requirement. A complete policy specification also requires a compensating change either in net government receipts or spending (or both). This section presents simulations for four such policies and their effects on the fiscal burdens of different generations.

The first of the four policies considered is a proposal to cut the social security payroll tax rate over the next three decades and to increase the tax rate thereafter. The second policy involves the same reduction in payroll taxes (through the year 2020) as in the first simulation, but rather than raise tax rates after 2020, this policy reduces social security benefits beginning in that year by the same amount that payroll taxes otherwise would have increased. The third policy entails the indirect dissipation of the social security trust fund though an increase in government spending over the next three decades equal, on an annual basis, to the social security surplus. Over these decades funds to pay for the increased government spending are "borrowed" so that in 2020 the additional accumulated federal debt is equal in magnitude to the social security trust fund. The fourth policy is an immediate and permanent switch from payroll tax finance to income tax finance of social security.

The first column of Table 2 indicates what reducing and then increasing payroll taxes will do to the burdens placed on different generations. The policy provides windfalls to Americans currently alive, with the exception of the very old and the very young. Those currently aged thirty to forty receive the largest windfalls, roughly $3,000 for males and $1,500 for females. These gains come at the expense of children currently under age ten as well as future individuals. If all future Americans are treated uniformly, up to the growth adjustment, their lifetime net payments will rise by $6,100, in the case of males, and $3,000, in the case of females.

Enactment of a policy that promises to raise future taxes to pay for current tax cuts does not ensure that such taxes will actually be raised. The government might use an alternative method to restore fiscal balance. For example, the necessary increase in net payments might take the form of a cut in social security benefits. Such a policy, depicted in the second column of Table 2, reduces by about one third for males and by about two thirds for females the gains enjoyed under the initial policy. Females lose relatively more because their share of social security benefits is larger than is their share of payroll tax payments.

The third column in Table 2 shows what happens if the federal govern-

TABLE 2.
Changes in Generational Accounts from Four Social Security Policies
(present value, thousands of dollars).

	Immediate payroll tax cuts financed by future tax increases	Immediate payroll tax cuts financed by benefit reductions	Dissipating the social security trust fund	Switching from payroll to income tax finance
Males				
Ages				
0	1.3	0.3	4.1	−2.4
10	−0.2	−0.6	4.0	−3.6
20	−2.3	−1.8	2.9	−4.4
30	−3.4	−2.2	1.5	−1.0
40	−3.2	−2.5	0.6	4.4
50	−2.0	−1.8	0.2	8.4
60	−0.7	−0.7	0	9.6
70	−0.1	−0.1	0	7.7
80	0	0	0	4.5
Future generations	6.1	3.8	5.2	−2.5
Females				
Ages				
0	0.6	0.4	1.9	−2.0
10	−0.3	−0.1	1.9	−3.1
20	−1.4	−0.6	1.5	−4.2
30	−1.7	−0.5	0.9	−2.0
40	−1.5	−0.6	0.4	1.3
50	−1.0	−0.5	0.1	4.2
60	−0.4	−0.4	0	5.6
70	0	0	0	4.8
80	0	0	0	2.2
Future generations	3.0	2.2	2.4	−2.2

ment indirectly dissipates the social security surplus by raising its spending beyond the amount projected in the baseline generational accounts. In the simulation, the government continues to accumulate its social security trust fund, but it also borrows to pay for additional spending with the annual amount of the borrowing equal in size to the annual social security surplus. We assume this process of deficit-financed increased spending continues through 2020, and that after 2020 the government raises income taxes to pay interest less an adjustment for growth on the additional accumulated official debt.

This policy has quite different effects from those in the previous simulations, since, unlike policies that do not change direct government spending, increases in government spending may eventuate in an increase in the sum of all generational accounts. Here, this added burden is borne by all generations who will be alive to service the extra debt, with the greatest burden on those currently young and those yet to be born. How this translates into the net impact on each generation depends on the size and distribution of the benefits of the added spending. Certainly if the benefits are spread over only those currently alive, the unborn will lose.

The final simulation in Table 2 shows the effects of a change in the method of financing social security benefits. Over the years some have argued that the connection between payroll taxes and OASDI benefits is sufficiently weak that there is little reason to rely on the payroll tax as a source of finance. The policy change considered here would replace the payroll tax with the income tax as the method of finance, immediately and permanently. Although such a change has been advocated for a variety of reasons, including a desire to use a more progressive source of revenue, our simulation considers only the generational effects of the switch. We find that those under forty stand to win, and those over forty stand to lose, because income taxes are levied on income from assets as well as income from labor, and older individuals receive a bigger share of asset income than labor income.

The generational implications of using general revenue finance to pay for social security are spelled out in the last column of Table 2. On average, sixty-year-old males and females would be forced to pay $9,600 and $5,600 more, respectively. Forty year-old males and females would suffer respective losses of $4,400 and $1,300. In contrast, males and females who are now age ten would benefit by more than $3,000 each. The policy also would represent more than a $2,000 lifetime net payment break to future generations.

In summary, the results in this table show that one cannot simply analyze the effects of a cut in payroll taxes; it is necessary to specify what replaces these taxes. The simulations suggest four possible routes: Increased payroll taxes in the future, reduced benefits in the future, reductions in government spending, and replacement with income taxes. Each has its own effects on the generational fiscal burden.

B. Medicare Policy

Many observers have worried about the rising level of health care costs in the United States, which spends a much larger fraction of GNP on health care than any other OECD country. After the United States, Canada is the country with the highest per capita health care spending, but the Canadians spend almost 30 percent less per person. At present, about $0.12 of every dollar of U.S. output goes to health care, compared with $0.06 in 1960. By the turn of the century the figure is projected to be $0.17. And if the growth of health care is unabated, the figure will reach $0.37 by the year 2030 (see Darman 1991).

What explains the rapid growth in real per capita U.S. health expenditures? Since 1960 slightly over half of the growth simply reflects expanded use of health care services and facilities. Another third of the growth is due to the price of medical care rising relative to the prices of other goods and services. And the remaining 11 or so percent of health expenditure growth reflects the aging of the population. This aging of America will, of course, intensify in the years ahead.

The growth of health care expenditures has potentially enormous implications for government outlays and the well-being of different generations. Consider just the federal government's expenditures on Medicare. These payments currently constitute 7 percent of total federal outlays. According to the Office of Management and Budget, Medicare is projected to exceed 30 percent of the federal budget by 2025. To support Medicare at its current levels alone, either the federal budget would have to grow far beyond its current level of about 20 percent of GNP or the rest of the budget would have to decline by more than 20 percent in real terms.

If Medicare's growth is not curtailed, how will its additional costs be financed? Given its cash-flow accounting, Medicare, like OASDI, will be reporting cash-flow surpluses over most of this decade as the HI (health insurance) component of payroll taxes grows. But by the end of the decade the higher payroll tax receipts will fall short of the increased Medicare spending, leading, in short order, to the exhaustion of the Medicare Trust Fund.

If and when the HI trust fund is dissipated, the government may raise payroll taxes, or may simply "borrow" from the OASI (Old Age Survivor Insurance) and DI (Disability Insurance) Social Security trust funds. Interfund social security borrowing has occurred in the past, and would delay the eventual need to raise payroll taxes, possibly until the burden of these higher taxes fell primarily on generations not yet born. According to Medicare's actuaries, the HI payroll tax may have to rise by anywhere from 6 to 16 percentage points. Because the combined employer-employee social security payroll tax is currently just over 15 percent, the uninhibited growth of Medicare expenditures could eventually require a doubling of social security taxes.

The generational accounts considered thus far were based on the assumption (perhaps naive) that medical expenditures will grow no faster than the rest of the economy. In light of the past growth of Medicare, Table 3 considers two alternative growth rates for Medicare expenditures over the 1990s. In the table Medicare outlays in the 1990s are assumed to grow at either a 2 or 4 percent higher rate than the rest of the economy. After the turn of the century the Medicare growth rate is assumed to equal the economy-wide growth rate. The 2 and 4 percent growth rates bracket the 2.77 rate of growth of health spending in excess of GNP observed between 1960 and 1989. The 4 percent growth rate is consistent with projections of an increase, over the decade, from 12 to 17 percent in the share of U.S. health care spending relative to GNP.

For each growth rate there are three alternative financing scenarios. The first is that future generations pick up the entire bill for this decade's projected higher Medicare growth. The second is that the growth in Medicare over the next decade is ultimately paid for by a reduction in Medicare benefits starting in the year 2020. The third is that this decade's growth in Medicare is matched, on an annual basis, with increases in HI payroll taxes.

The three scenarios have markedly different implications for both living and unborn generations. Under the first scenario, the burden is entirely shifted onto future generations; all living generations benefit from the growth in Medicare, because they do not have to pay for it. Depending on the growth rate assumed, future generations end up paying from 10 to 23 percent more than in the base case. If Medicare growth is 4 percent, the absolute increase in the bill handed to our male descendants is $19,400; it is $9,000 for our female descendants. These additional burdens raise substantially the ratio of total net payments of the unborn to those of newborns. Rather than paying 21 percent more than newborns, future generations in the 4 percent growth scenario end up paying almost 50 percent more than newborns.

The second scenario, given in columns 2 and 5, indicates what happens if, instead of borrowing from the Social Security Trust Fund, Medicare pays for its prospective near-term generosity with longer-term (after 2020) benefit cuts. In this case, individuals below age fifty lose, because of the net cuts in Medicare benefits in their retirement. Note also that today's older individuals experience the same large gains from Medicare growth as in the previous financing scenario for the simple reason that, by assumption, the projected Medicare benefit cuts do not begin for thirty years.

The third financing mechanism, which involves annual increases in HI payroll taxes to pay for the excess Medicare growth, is explored in Columns 3 and 6. This scenario hurts an even larger fraction of those alive, but has the smallest effect on members of future generations, whose net payments rise by roughly the same proportion as those for individuals age thirty and under. As in the previous cases, members of older generations, who have essentially retired and ceased paying payroll taxes, enjoy roughly the same gain from the near-term growth in Medicare.

Given the persistent growth of health care costs, one might ask how much more extreme these results would be if Medicare spending grew as a share of GNP not for the next decade but, say, for the next three decades. We repeated the simulations in Table 3 under the assumption

TABLE 3.

*Changes in Generational Accounts from Medicare Policies
(present value, thousands of dollars).*

	2 percent growth rate			4 percent growth rate		
	Future generations pay	Eventual Medicare benefit cut	Pay-as-you-go finance	Future generations pay	Eventual Medicare benefit cut	Pay-as you-go finance
Males						
Ages						
0	−0.2	0.1	1.6	−0.5	0.3	3.4
10	−0.4	0.2	2.1	−0.9	0.5	4.6
20	−0.6	0.4	2.3	−1.4	0.8	4.9
30	−1.0	0.7	1.6	−2.2	1.6	3.6
40	−1.6	0.1	0.4	−3.5	0.1	0.7
50	−2.7	−1.9	−1.6	−5.9	−4.2	−3.5
60	−4.2	−4.2	−3.9	−9.2	−9.2	−8.5
70	−3.6	−3.6	−3.5	−7.7	−7.7	−7.5
80	−2.0	−2.0	−2.0	−4.3	−4.3	−4.3
Future generations	8.9	3.3	2.0	19.4	7.1	4.3
Females						
Ages						
0	−0.3	0.2	0.7	−0.7	0.4	1.5
10	−0.5	0.3	0.9	−1.2	0.7	1.9
20	−0.8	0.5	0.7	−1.8	1.1	1.5
30	−1.3	0.9	0	−2.9	2.0	0
40	−2.1	0.3	−1.2	−4.7	0.6	−2.6
50	−3.5	−2.0	−3.0	−7.8	−4.5	−6.6
60	−5.5	−5.5	−5.3	−11.9	−11.9	−11.6
70	−4.9	−4.9	−4.9	−10.7	−10.7	−10.6
80	−2.9	−2.9	−2.9	−6.2	−6.2	−6.2
Future generations	4.2	1.8	0.8	9.0	3.8	1.9

that Medicare grows at a rate 2 percent or 4 percent faster than GNP until 2020. Not surprisingly, the burden on future generations grows considerably under these assumptions, but the extent of this growth depends on the policy being simulated. If Medicare costs rise at a rate 2 percent faster than GNP and benefits are eventually cut (in 2020), the added burden on future males would rise from $3,300 to $12,600; that on females from $1,800 to $6,000. At the other extreme, the "worst case" scenario is when Medicare grows at a 4% faster rate until 2020, and only future generations pay. In this case, the added burden on future males rises from $19,400 to $62,100, that on females from $9,000 to $26,200. Given that our baseline simulations assign future males and females **total** fiscal burdens of $89,500 and $44,200, respectively, we see that sustained Medicare growth has the potential of absorbing a significant share of the government's overall budget.

VI. CONCLUSION

We have estimated that the United States' policy path, based on current law and the assumption of balanced growth in government spending, will place a roughly 21 percent larger growth-adjusted net tax burden on future generations than it will place on Americans who have recently been born. But this estimate is based on what may be relatively optimistic assumptions: That the social security system's projected cash-flow surpluses will continue to accumulate and that Medicare spending will immediately stabilize as a share of GNP. Those individuals coming in the future as well as today's infants and young children could end up paying considerably more under less optimistic but realistic alternative paths for social security and Medicare policies.

Specifying a different path for payroll taxes or Medicare costs is not enough to describe an alternative fiscal policy: one must also indicate how the government will compensate for either of these changes in order to preserve intertemporal fiscal balance. Though we know some balancing response **must** occur, the ultimate path cannot, of course, be known with certainty; we have considered several alternatives in each case.

The social security policies we have analyzed include short-term payroll tax cuts financed by long-term payroll tax increases, future benefit cuts, or general revenue finance, as well as the dissipation of the impending social security "off-budget" surpluses through increased "on-budget" deficits. Our simulations for Medicare consider alternative responses to the continued growth of Medicare expenditures as a share of GNP. The use of generational accounting reveals, as deficit accounting cannot, the relative burdens that these different policy responses place on different generations.

REFERENCES

Auerbach, Alan J., Jagadeesh Gokhale, and Laurence J. Kotlikoff (1991). "Generational Accounts: A Meaningful Alternative to Deficit Accounting." In *Tax Policy and the Economy*. David Bradford, ed. National Bureau of Economic Research, vol. 5, 55–110.

—— (1992). "Generational Accounting—A New Approach to Understanding the Effects of Fiscal Policy on Saving." *Scandinavian Journal of Economics,* forthcoming.

Bohn, Henning (1991). "The Sustainability of Budget Deficits in a Stochastic Economy." Working paper, Wharton School, University of Pennsylvania, July.

Darman, Richard (1991). "Introductory Statement: The Problem of Rising Health Costs." Testimony presented before the Senate Finance Committee, Executive Office of the President, Office of Management and Budget, April 16, p. 6.

Kotlikoff, Laurence J. (1992). *Generational Accounting—Knowing Who Pays, and When, for What We Spend.* New York: The Free Press, forthcoming.